Zen Master
Next Door

Zen Master
Next Door

Parables for Enlightened Everyday Living

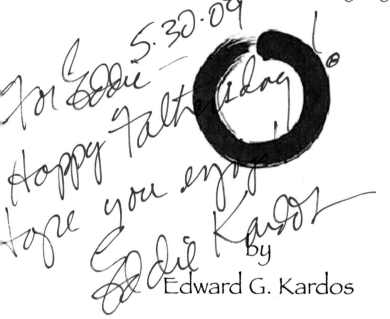

by

Edward G. Kardos

Humanics Publishing Group
Atlanta, Georgia; Lake Worth, Florida

This book is a work of fiction.
Places, events and situations in this book are purely fictional.
Any resemblance to actual persons, living or dead is coincidental.

For My Father
The Original Eddie Zen

Contents

Acknowledgements

Although a writer travels a solitary path, true accomplishments are the making of many. This is evident in the culmination of Zen Master Next Door.

For reading my original manuscript and pushing it forward, I'm thankful to acquisitions editor, W. Arthur Bligh. For taking a risk and offering superb guidance along the way, I want to thank my publisher, Gary Wilson. David Ziegler, my copy editor, took my thoughts and words and gave them clarity and precision. For her wonderful cover and book design, and especially her patience, thanks goes to Marcia Karasoff. I appreciate the talents of all those I worked with at Humanics, especially Jane and her help during the process.

Author Dean King saw value in my earlier writings and inspired me to move forward on this project. I owe much to my long time friend, Fred Jolly. I owe a debt of gratitude to my late friend Frank Griffith who left me with much to think about and practice in my own life. I wish to thank Larry Masters who read the early version of these stories and ratcheted up my confidence level, insisting he wanted to see my work in print. I thank my friend Blake MacIver for his genuine interest and the stories we shared.

So many people gave me fodder for my thoughts: my parents, the old man up the street when I was a kid, the lady who used to chase me out of her yard as I walked home from school, the mechanics I met, my teachers, my neighbors and the guy who lives two street over. I would be remiss not to thank the acquaintances, as well as strangers, who have come and gone in my life, all sharing with me something new—something real.

Thanks go to my whole family, but mostly to my children, who have already heard what a reader will find in the following pages. To Zach, Stephanie, Mary and Elizabeth: you have taught me well. Most of all, and with deep and abiding appreciation, I thank my loving wife Kristin, who provided the litmus test for my stories, and the encouragement she offered when I needed it most.

Preface

I remember a day a few years back, while driving home, when the sun was bright, and the volume on my car radio was up a few extras notches. I was totally at ease singing the song on the radio as onlookers in other cars smiled, while others poked fun. But most, I observed, didn't even notice my frivolity as their cell phones appeared to be permanently affixed to their ears. This, I discovered, was usual as I stopped at traffic lights, one after the other, and gazed at the passengers of neighboring vehicles. They were in cars, vans and trucks next to me but they weren't really there. I remember a time when driving gave us a respite from ringing phones and daily demands. There was a time when paying attention to the road was important—maybe I shouldn't have been singing.

I thought about this situation. What I decided was that those people, who depend on so many external gizmos to get through their days, need to do more for themselves. I thought that if only they listened to the yarn within them. Why are WE so attached to things? Things, I think in the scheme of things are terribly unimportant. If we listen to ourselves, we begin to realize what's important. If we listen to others we might find answers instead of avoiding them. If we contemplated these questions, couldn't we become more enlightened?

Some of what's important, in my estimation, comes out in stories: all of humanity strives for the same things. We are connected, and we are all spiritual beings, regardless of our faith tradition. We find out that the sacred is in the ordinary. We find that we are a compassionate people—we must be.

In stories, we discover that we understand ourselves and, in doing so, we understand others. My writing that became Zen Master Next Door is a tool for me to share. What seems so obvious to all of us may be so thorny, at best, to reach. These stories are relevant and timely as we yearn to live an inspired life. Parables explore age-old ideas, but are germain as we detach ourselves from what is unquestionably unimportant, distracting and troublesome. Between us and the truth is a nasty thicket, but one that, with the correct gear, is easily attainable. One tool may be, in fact, being able to recognize the "Zen Master" who may be as close to us as next door.

We can look within ourselves and see our reflection within these parables. Zen Master Next Door aims to show each of us that we can find similar stories of inspiration within ourselves. In each parable, my hope is that the reader contemplates how each character and each circumstance relates to their own lives. We all possess great stories of enlightenment to share.

These parables are based in truth and on real occurrences, but are the epitome of fiction—the guts of storytelling are the essence of truth. They are gentle but strong. They embrace but let go. They are simple and complex.

They are, of course, parables.

Edward G. Kardos
September 15, 2008

Share your stories with the author
by connecting with him on his web site at
www.edwardgkardos.com.

LISTENING TO

ACQUAINTANCES

EDDIE ZEN

The energy of the mind is the essence of life.
– Aristotle

Listen to the voice of nature, for it holds treasures for you.
– Huron—Native American

When knowledge becomes tattered, wisdom springs.
– Eddie Zen

The best place to start is with the truth. At least that's what he told Judd, his neighbor of nearly a decade.

"Answers to questions most important to humanity always lie within us. Come on, certainly you've heard that before," Eddie said with a frothy tone. He was known to start conversations this way, bypassing any normal greeting.

On a warm breeze that filtered through the trees in Eddie's front yard, arrived the rich fragrance of juniper from Judd's garden next door. The two men were alone although surrounded by houses. Speckled with boxes, chairs, tables and bookcases, this once pristine postage stamp-sized lot now resembled a yard sale but without the swarms of bargain hunters.

Judd had dropped by on a lark, not knowing that his elderly neighbor was moving that very day. But that was common practice for both men; Judd was unaware of much around him, while Eddie was unpredictable at best.

Replying to the older man, Judd nodded his head. "What's going on here? Where are you going?"

"I'm moving on... just moving on. But don't worry about that, because

I'm trying to give you something to think about. What I want you to know is that answers you are in search of come from wisdom passed through the ages. I repeat, in case you aren't catching on, it's about *wisdom* — *w-i-s-d-o-m*."

Giving in as he usually did, Judd said, "all right already; so where does it come from? This wisdom."

"Good question," Eddie said, drawing in a slow breath while scratching his day old stubble. "It started with our first ancestors and flowed on year after year, decade after decade and century after... well you get my point. It just has to be, well unless some of us got here riding in some kind of space-ship from Mars or some such place," he said, squinting as he looked to the gray, hazy sky, thick with summer's humidity. "Anyway, although this wis-dom has been fermented like a good Chardonnay many times over for many years, it is now tucked away. Seldom does modern man give it much weight."

Eddie sat down on a dusty, wooded trunk and yanked off his horn-rimmed glasses. He held them up, saw a smudge or two, and put them back on. Taking a long, deliberate breath, he continued. "Today we rely more on science at one end of the spectrum or blind faith at the other. Wisdom is overlooked and seldom part of our decision making. Don't you think?" he asked, expecting only a head nod. Judd obliged.

As the movers in the house packed Eddie's belongings, it dawned on Judd that he was always drawn to Eddie's musings and now seeing him leave the neighborhood, an instant sense of emptiness plopped in his abdomen. With downcast eyes, Judd told him that he wished he had taken the time to get to know him—to *really* know him.

What Judd did know was that his neighbor was a rather imposing but gentle man. Standing a hair over six feet tall, he was slender and looked like a man ten years his junior. He always donned frayed oxford shirts which draped on his torso like bed linens on a grandmother's clothesline. His silver hair was thick for a man of any age, impeccably combed and parted to the side with the straightest of parts.

Eddie's easy smile and radiant disposition unwittingly drew Judd to him and always did. Despite his incessant ramblings, Judd knew Eddie was a singular sort. A ready smile punctuated Eddie's discourse, whether it was a smile showing his exceptionally white teeth or his pursed-lipped version that underscored his points along the way.

"Ah, you know me well enough. Don't worry about that. Get to know yourself! Get to know others and learn from them. Get to know the guy next door. This is what I'm talking about," he told Judd, springing from his seat and walking to a lopsided pyramid of boxes.

He began fumbling through a crumbling, corrugated container. Silence was seldom experienced when in Eddie's company, though for the moment he fell quiet, looking perplexed as he shuffled papers in the container. Losing his concentration from moment to moment, he would pause as he examined an ancient fountain pen or a softball-sized sphere of rubber bands.

"Are you looking for something?" Judd asked.

"Yes. Why, what does it look like I'm doing?" he said with a sigh. "It's in here somewhere. I want to give you something I started and I insist you finish it. What I'm looking for will show you what I mean."

Eddie continued to rummage through boxes. As he did, dust emanated from each box flap, filling the immediate area with a ripe tang.

Eddie stopped for a moment, looking up without his signature gleam. "You've always been kind to me and listened as I've spouted off at the first moment you've gotten home from work and are kind enough to speak with me while you're out in the yard. Even at last year's Fourth of July block party, I pulled you away from the beer cooler to throw you a thought, and you were there with a catcher's mitt to snare it. Whatever I threw out there, you were willing to give it the kind of attention I was looking for." He smiled and nodded as if proud of a son.

Judd, always neatly dressed and clean shaven, was in his late thirties, had a muscular physique and short-cropped blonde curls with steely blue eyes. His usual look was a golf shirt, khaki shorts and flip-flops. He was always pleasant and kind.

Married to Ashley for nine years, Judd had two children. Rarely taking time to think beneath the facade of many issues, Judd spent time taking care of his young family with little time for introspection. He wasn't so different than most folks. Eddie knew this.

Judd couldn't imagine what he was hunting for, and as Eddie rifled through dusty boxes, he suddenly felt empty-handed, wanting to reciprocate. He thought of nothing of worth that he could conjure up to give the old man. This worried him. Judd told him that.

Preoccupied while looking through his belongings, Eddie gently gestured to him, waving his hands in the air while saying, "You've given me plenty. But, I guess you don't realize that, now do you?"

Before Judd could utter a syllable and from calm to excitement and without warning, Eddie blurted, "Ah, yes, eureka! Here it is!"

Before rescuing the gift from the box, Eddie peered down at what he was in search of. There was a glow about his eyes. He took a breath and pulled it up and out. As if it was a gold brick, he handed Judd a ream of yellowed paper, tattered and dog-eared at many of the edges. Tinged with a scent of mildew, what Eddie held, Judd knew, was significant. As Eddie flipped through and peered at many of the pages, Judd saw that what he was handing him was a collection of handwritten stories.

Taken by the gesture, Judd asked, "Why are you giving these to me? I mean, this looks like a lifetime of work. You ought to keep them." At best he was bewildered.

Eddie put his hand in his pockets and, leaning forward on his toes, explained, "I don't need them where I'm going. Besides, my hands can no longer tolerate holding a pen for very long. Perhaps you can read them and put them to good use in some way. Maybe it'll get you off your duff and get you to write something too. You know it's in you! It's a gift-- it's not polite to ask questions... by the way, they're parables."

Overheated from his search, Eddie sat in a recliner that had been plunked down under a maple tree in his front yard, waiting for just the right time to be loaded onto the moving van. He looked up intently at the massive tree boughs, and it gave him pleasure as his thoughts accompanied the expression of resolve on his face. He motioned to Judd to pull up a kitchen chair from the mountain of boxes on the other side of the slate walkway, and to join him.

In the fashion of Socrates dispensing philosophies under an olive tree, Eddie began to expound. "When we read stories, you know, it is natural for us to pull personal meaning from them. This in itself is a good thing. Don't you think? Writers like it when this happens. As I like to think, it may lead to introspection—I like that word. But at the very least stories help us think. Are you with me?"

Judd was a trifle confused. "So what is it all about? I mean, you always tell me that the answers are inside of each of us. Is that what you have written about? The answers you have found in you?"

With his long, thin finger pointing to his own chest, Eddie answered. "Precisely. I did say that, but it doesn't mean I know all the answers. In complexity there is simplicity. In simplicity there is complexity. Answers aren't always the result of equations or any logical order—if so, we would unfetter all the mysteries and be superhumans and not, well, just humans. There's nothing perfect about any one of us. I do, however, think that stories, not just mine, are like beautiful sunflowers. They hold beliefs and values that somehow creep and root themselves into most civilizations. Like a tall sunflower staring us in the face we sometimes still ask—where?"

The workmen were moving his life's possessions with such disturbing ease. "This move shouldn't be this easy and this fast," Judd thought. Eddie saluted the movers as they filed by him. The yard and the house had begun to empty.

In spite of the commotion around him, Judd began to think of all the times he and Eddie had talked in the past and he was only now beginning to connect the dots: the excuses Eddie made by walking over to Judd's house, ringing the doorbell to borrow a dictionary. "Eddie needs a dictionary? How come I didn't think that was odd," Judd scolded himself. He thought of the times that Eddie would show up with a beer in hand when Judd cooked burgers on the grill, or wanted to borrow a snow shovel in May. These were times that Eddie had something to say. Sometimes Judd listened and other times he was preoccupied. "I wish I had been present all those times," Judd thought.

Eddie continued, "We're all the same... We're all the same. The mores and ways of life are probed and pondered today just as they were by those who resided at Stonehenge, or by the ancient Greeks, or the Bushmen of Africa or the contemporaries of Confucius, or the greeter at Wal-Mart or the neighbor over the fence, or me or you. Did I leave out anyone? By and large, these truths are worthy of another look, don't you think? Perhaps two or three more looks. That's all I'm saying."

As Judd looked away for a moment and turned back to answer, Eddie seemed to have vanished. Scanning the yard, Judd noticed that Eddie was slowly climbing the front steps of his home to determine the progress of the workers. Judd stayed, enjoying the warmth of Eddie's lingering presence. Although it was getting close to noon and hotter than ever, he was content as he imagined what the old man was all about. He began flipping through the ragged paper and found himself easing back into the recliner. He thumbed through the musty pages, reading snippets of different stories and passages. He found himself mesmerized.

Judd put the bundle of papers on his lap, took a breath, got up, and began to search for Eddie. More questions swirled in his head.

Eddie walked to the rear of the house, orchestrating the movers. Judd caught up with him and followed.

After a moment, Eddie pulled himself away from the mundane and, in awkward silence, walked to the main staircase six feet from his opened front door. He sat down on the eighth step. He crossed his legs at his boney ankles and placed his graceful hands to the back of his head. Sunbeams shot through the door. With one eye closed, he squinted the other and surveyed the goings on in the front yard to assess what was left to be loaded.

Peering from side to side, he saw that each room was empty. He stood and then moved with a lightened gait, as if a burden was being lifted from his shoulders. He walked outside and down the brick stoop one last time.

Judd picked up his pace to join him in the front of the house. The movers were busy repositioning the recliner in the recesses of the truck. Nothing was left to pack or load. With a yank of a canvas strap, the back door of the truck slammed shut. Just like that, his belongings were stowed away, never to return.

Eddie shouted, "Remember to deliver the furniture and boxes that are marked in red and send the rest on to the Salvation Army." The men nodded and Eddie waved them on. He turned back to Judd.

"My parables, if you can call them that, are an attempt to show that there is meaning in all the ordinary things we do. Life lessons can be learned wherever we are, whether in a bustling city, on a farm in America's heartland, or in a suburban neighborhood. There is much we can learn from the taxi driver, the stock broker, the dairy farmer and the neighborhood hairdresser. I've learned a thing or two from her over the years," he said smugly. He sighed, placing his hand on Judd's shoulder. "In a way, they teach us who we are. Wisdom is not only right in front of us—it is within us. The truth that evades us lies within. It always has."

The moment fell silent. Eddie turned to look at his house one more time. He faced Judd and with a toothy smile he implored, "don't you feel it?"

A moment later he walked to his car, got in, and still smiling, he waved to Judd. Judd reciprocated.

"I'll visit," Judd said.

"No you won't. You don't know where I'm headed. Do me one better."

"What's that?"

"Look inside and add the next chapter."

With that, Eddie drove away, not waiting for his neighbor's response. Judd's mind was empty and said nothing. Mum, he stood. But when Eddie was out of sight, his mind was now replete, and silently bade him a farewell with a promise.

"Goodbye Eddie. I will."

The Kingdom of God is within you.

— Jesus

Be a lamp to yourself. Be your own confidence. Hold to the truth within yourself, as to the only truth.

— The Buddha

In the attitude of silence the soul finds the path in a clearer light, and what is elusive and deceptive resolves itself into crystal clearness. Our life is a long and arduous quest after the Truth.

– Gandhi

Seek not good from without; seek it within yourself, or you will never find it.

– Epictetus—second century

Ask questions from your heart and you will be answered for the heart.

– Omaha—Native American

———— ⋙⋘ ————

Sometimes it takes storytelling to convince any spiritual being what he or she should already know. Truth comes from within. Simple? Maybe, but truth leads to wisdom which is the tenuous center amid science and faith. What is truth? Who is truth? We must pause to discern how truth is real and part of our daily lives. But it's not enough to know oneself. As truth lies beneath our bones so it lies beneath our neighbor's bones as well. Simple?

———— ⋙⋘ ————

A GOOD MAN

If you want others to be happy, practice compassion. If you want to be happy, practice compassion.

— Dalai Lama

Let us be the ones who say we do not accept that a child dies every three seconds simply because he does not have the drugs you and I have. Let us be the ones to say we are not satisfied that your place of birth determines your right to life. Let us be outraged, let us be loud, let us be bold.

— Brad Pitt

Clifton, his wife Mary Katherine and their small children, Tristan and Blair, lived in a neighborhood with sprawling lawns and irrigation systems that resembled fountains when in use. Neighbors separated themselves with serpentine walls that clearly delineated what belonged to whom. Like small islands, each yard, wall and fence finely declared each home's sovereignty, independent from neighborhood and community. Focus, in all its subtle and not-so-subtle aspects, was entirely inward.

Possessions, either the abundance of or the lack thereof, have a way of shaping consciousness. For the neighborhood's residents, purchases were frequent and large. Life, as it seemed, was easy for most. Perhaps access to credit and a resignation to indebtedness allowed for such fortresses, as most of those who dwelled in the neighborhood came from much humbler beginnings.

Clifton and his family were no different. Clifton had toiled for years as a lawyer, climbing the corporate ladder, working late nights, skipping vacations, and sacrificing many of the joys of parenthood to provide an abundant life for his family. His work, to all appearances, had paid off, as he would soon be named a partner at one of the most prominent and prestigious law firms downtown.

For a man in his early forties, Clifton Haywood appeared to be slightly older than his years. Brooks Brothers suits, custom-tailored dress shirts, and the finest silk ties adorned his walk-in closet, which, in some countries, could house a small family. His sideburns were already silver and his crown was barely covered by only a few of the hardiest strands of hair. Enjoying any cuisine that met his inclination, and not seeing the inside of a gym for some time, he toted extra capacity around his midsection. Despite his physical characteristics, his outstanding posture presented a confident, regal demeanor. Only his shoes evidenced more polish than his manner.

—————

While Clifton's self-assured air of achievement seemed inherent and ancestral, he wasn't always a successful lawyer. He didn't always live in a province of sorts. And he didn't always maintain a regal demeanor. Clifton grew up in a modest suburb outside of Pittsburgh and, at age 22, headed south for law school at the College of William and Mary. Reared by hard-working, blue- collar parents, he became interested in law during dinner table conversations he had with his father and mother.

"Whatever you do, Cliff, do what is right and just—show you have compassion," his father said frequently.

Cliff, as he was known in his younger days, didn't realize that his Dad spoke from his own experiences, working in the steel mills while making ends meet for his growing family. Bullied and most times powerless, his dad worked many years in horrifying conditions with little or no voice. His father did what he had to do for his family. Cliff's parents, by most accounts, were good people.

—————

Clifton's hardworking ethic was lauded by his peers. He booked more billable hours than most in his firm and took cases that stretched him and his colleagues. The first eight years out of law school, Clifton's *pro bono* work was acclaimed by not-for-profit organizations that greatly benefited from his dedication. His success with high-dollar cases was equally profound, garnering frequent praise from firm shareholders.

Once his indelible mark at the firm had been made, Clifton thought less of those days as a kid who listened attentively to his undereducated folks at the dinner table. The blurring of the years and the stressors of his profession, compounded by the pressure of raising his children, had made Clifton more insular, heightening his interest in the benefits of wealth. He always knew the need for justice with compassion, but thought more about chalking up, again and again, more "victories" for the firm. More and more, ego had begun to shape his actions. But Clifton knew this, and in spite of his shift in focus, he, under layers of crust, was still Cliff, and could only be thought of as a good man.

Despite a childhood of private schools and country clubs, Mary Katherine's primary focus was family. She made sure that the Haywoods spent quality time with each other. She volunteered at the children's school, encouraging Clifton to carve out time in his schedule to attend school concerts and be "mystery reader" for Blair's first grade classmates. She was the Brownie leader and Clifton was Cub Scout leader—and they enjoyed themselves. They spent "alone time" one night a week dining out. The family attended Catholic Church often and was generous when the collection plate was passed. By every account, they were considered good people.

———

Good people, like anyone else, sometimes do a poor job of looking beyond what's immediately important to them. The Haywoods knew their neighbors next door, but beyond, others were merely acquaintances. The neighborhood was full of "wavers," and everyone seemed to participate. As Clifton inspected his yard, he would wave to the walkers he would spot. Neighbors driving by each other would extend a cordial wave. Children biking up and down the street knew to wave as well. It was a most congenial, yet deeply distant, group.

Such was the case with Sally O'Hara. Sally lived five houses down from the Haywoods, on the other side of the street. She and her late husband, Ben, were the original owners of their home, built in 1955. She had seen countless families come and go. When Sally and Ben had first moved in, neighbors made a point of getting to know each other. That was another time.

Sally's home was much like the others, with a great deal of property and beautifully landscaped. A product of old family wealth, she was able to hire landscapers to keep up the place, especially her front yard. Gardening in her private backyard made her happy.

She was seventy-four, without children, and seldom did a visitor come to call on her. Her driveway and garage were off the back of her home, so neighbors did not see her coming nor going with any regularity. She kept to herself—a phantom to those only a few houses away.

Sally was roughly five feet four inches when she felt well. Her thin hair was white like cotton balls but frizzy, allowing her scalp to show. Her eyes were hazel with an abundance of green flecks, and the lines on her face, seemed to tell stories, each line leading someplace and to someone. She was comfortable in kimonos and other loosely flowing, but colorful clothes.

Over the years, a variety of rumors had surfaced about Sally, whether from parents at their children's bus stop, or during the few times that her neighbors convened at neighborhood association meetings to discuss important items, like the approved heights of shrubs or colors for homes. To the chagrin of many, at Halloween, Sally festooned her house with eerie decoration, wittingly playing up the lore. The common view was that she was an eccentric, bitter recluse, but some neighbors agreed that she could be friendly, as she was amiable when she mixed with them on rare occasions. No one dared, or truly cared, to learn much more about Mrs. O'Hara. They, like Clifton and Mary Katherine, were happy in their own worlds. Nevertheless, the neighbors, in all appearances, were good people.

—∞—

It was one of those days that the leaves swirled in tiny cyclones in a hodgepodge of crimson and ginger, leaving the heat of summer behind and the cool gusts of fall impelling, among many things, fresh attitudes of the end of the year. Clifton, sitting at the desk in his downtown office, had begun the chilly morning by keeping his eye on his unusually hot cup of coffee, waiting for it to cool before he attempted to bring it to his lips.

The phone rang, jarring him.

"Hello, Mr. Haywood. This is Mrs. O'Hara."

Giving little attention to the person on the other end of the phone, Clifton began to multi-task, signing documents and shuffling other papers as he was clueless to whom he was talking. Upon completing her introduction, it dawned on him that this was in fact the voice of his reclusive neighbor. She sounded younger than what he would expect. Her voice was clear and melodic. She was upbeat but austere, carefully choosing her next words.

"Oh, hello, Mrs. O'Hara. How are you?"

"I'm dying."

Stunned by her response, Clifton struggled to regain his composure.

"Mrs. O'Hara, do you need immediate help?"

"No, no. I've got some time yet, but I want to meet with you. Can you come by my house on Thursday afternoon?"

Knowing he was busy Thursday, Clifton heard dread in her voice and he sensed a queasiness in the pit of his gut; he immediately felt compelled to reshuffle his day. Her tone and frankness resonated with Clifton, warming his heart. He remembered his *pro bono* days.

"Why yes Mrs. O'Hara, I would be happy to. What is it you would like me to do?" he said calmly.

Clifton received his answer with the murmur of a dial tone. Doing his best to shrug it off, he assumed that she had phoned him because he was a lawyer and could help her get her estate in order. "But why me?," he thought. She apparently has money. He conjured up many suppositions, in the end concluding that she must have squandered her assets when her husband died. All his thoughts pointed to the idea that she really needed him.

Clifton pushed away from his ornate, mahogany desk, stood up from his stiff, high-back executive chair, and pivoted on his right heel to face the gigantic windows overlooking the rest of the gray and white concrete of the city. From seventeen flights up, he could see for miles. What he saw was the world. This is where he seemed safest.

Thursday came like it was the next hour. He hurried his work to make sure that he could get out of the city and back to his neighborhood without being late. Being on time was paramount. He assumed that she would expect that of him. Anxious that morning, he had knocked over his coffee on his desk—something he had never done before.

Checking the time on his cell phone, Clifton found himself standing on Mrs. O'Hara's front porch precisely on time. He rang the doorbell and wait-ed. With a gasp or two, he began to feel impatient. He loosened his tie only slightly since the pulse in his neck was pronounced. Checking himself over, he noticed a few tiny coffee stains on his gold silk tie. He felt like walking away.

After what seemed to be five minutes, she cautiously opened the door. He expected to hear a creak, but none was to be heard. Like a magnet, Clifton's bloodshot eyes met hers. They were engaging. Silently, she motioned him to come in. This tranquil and wordless introduction allowed his nerves to settle. As he entered her home, she asked if he could leave his shoes at the door. Taken by surprise, he nodded with a faint smile and slipped off his wingtips, only then remembering that he had a nuisance of a hole in his sock at his right heel.

Gently reaching for his arm, Sally tugged him, and they moved to the living room, where she asked him to sit. Clifton wasn't used to such hospi-tality, but welcomed her advance.

Sally was barefoot and wearing a traditional and colorful Ethiopian dress. Silver bracelets rose up her freckled wrists and many of her fingers were ornamented with rings of different shapes and styles. The color of her mani-cured nails matched her lips. She was elegant.

Clifton scanned his surroundings, immediately noticing that the home was furnished and decorated like none he had ever seen. There was nothing noticeably strange or out of place. In fact, the quality of the decorations, from her Impressionism paintings to the figurines gracing her many built in bookcases, was staggering. He expected something different; perhaps cats and a lot of them. But, now that he thought about it, he really hadn't known what to expect.

A peculiar scent loomed in the air; it was a combination of tea, and incense. Although it was not a common fragrance, it was soothing. Clifton sat down in an overstuffed chair and she offered him green tea that was already on a side table. He sat back and sipped the tea as she poured a cup for herself. Thinking of his morning coffee mishap, he relished the aroma and fine taste of the tea. He had forgotten how he liked tea. During this lull, he found himself carefully studying the tea cups. They had an interesting shape, like a cone. The outside of the cup and the pot had an Asian design that was unfamiliar to him. He knew it wasn't a Target or Wal-Mart purchase.

Sally made herself comfortable on a companion chair directly in front of him. Their knees were only about six inches from touching each other. Like waves in the ocean, his nerves went from ease to unease. Clifton was accustomed to feeling his large bulky wooden desk between him and his clients.

Sally was quick to smile as she settled herself into her chair. Preoccupied with her eyes, Clifton couldn't decide why they were so enthralling. This was the first time he had seen her up close. From a distance, people seem generic, plain, and easy to stereotype. Today he saw her differently.

With only sounds of sipping, Sally broke the near quiet with a question. "Did I tell you I was dying?"

"Why yes, you did."

"You know you are dying, too?"

With this rejoinder, Clifton at once thought that all the rumors must be true. He was sipping tea with a nutcase.

"But I'm dying a bit faster than you, I suppose, because I will be gone by the first snow. That's what I want to talk to you about."

Clifton's mood shifted away from his acute frustration and relaxed the best he could. He always did his best when he controlled his mood. The conversation was anything but clear, so he didn't honestly know how to react. He hesitated, finally responding with a pursed lip and deliberate, understanding nod. He was trying not to form a judgment.

Sally continued. "I've noticed you for a few years. You're a good man and I humor myself by thinking I'm a good judge of character. I really don't give a rat's you-know-what about your profession or social standing. Sorry to be so blunt, but character is important and, at this point in my life, you being a lawyer is a plus."

Clifton sat a little taller in his chair, eyes lighting up. He began to feel more comfortable as Sally began to provide more flesh to the mere bones she originally gave to him.

Still not totally knowing how to handle the situation, Clifton replied to her as if he were talking with his own father.

"Thank you. I always try to do my best."

"See, that's what I mean. Your ego is well in check, I can tell. I don't want to contend with a pompous you-know-what. I want to talk with a person I can trust who will help me. I know I can trust you—I just know that, but only you can answer the question; do you want to help me?"

"Why yes I do. I can help you. I do *pro bono* work."

Sally's face darkened. She leaned forward, eyes aflame. Careful not to wag her index finger, she instead wagged all five, responding, "Cut that thought right now. I'm not looking for a freebie. I'm talking about helping me. Yes, your knowledge can help me, but I don't want to be a charity case. I can afford any lawyer in town. ANY lawyer." Calming herself down and with a forced smile, she continued, "I'll ask again. Do you want to help me?"

Clifton had never been asked this question with the same audaciousness than that of Mrs. O'Hara.

"Yes, I now understand. I *do* want and will help you."

"*She wants MY help*," Clifton thought. "*She's pissed when I tell her I'll help her for free, and she's asking me to help her but she tortures me telling me nothing other than she's dying—I must have missed an important day in law school.*"

"Thank you. Please follow me," Sally said. Clifton knew she liked control, but so did he. However, at this point his interest was sufficiently piqued. Perhaps it was best to let her call the shots and for him to listen.

After teetering back and forth a few times, Clifton pulled himself up from the chair. They walked to the rear of the house to a larger, cramped room filled with framed photos, plaques, news clippings and an assortment of memorabilia. This was the origin of the burning incense he had smelled. It was a virtual museum of Sally and her late husband, spanning half a century. Strangely, none of the myriad of impressive plaques, honors or commemorations were displayed on a wall or on shelves. Instead, they were stacked in corners, under tables and in other obscure places throughout the room.

What hung prominently on the walls were photos of countless faces of all shapes, colors and sizes—people she met during her long life. There were photographs, drawings and homemade paintings of people. Children, the elderly and young adults—most were clearly smiling, while some were being comforted by others. There were scenes of people working, learning and praying. They were everywhere, covering every surface of every wall. Upon more examination, Clifton felt it wasn't a museum but, in fact, hallowed ground. What he saw was humanity. What was cherished was humanity. The eyes in the photographs told stories much like that of Sally.

"Wow. May I take a look around?"

"Yes, go ahead."

Clifton slowly plodded around the room, gazing at the many pictures. He noticed, with great veneration, that she was in some of the pictures. "Look at how young she is. Mrs. O'Hara must be thirty years old in some of these," he thought. It was the eyes that gave her away in the pictures. They showed a happiness and serenity not commonly seen. Most were candid shots of her feeding babies, toting buckets of water, or, in one particular photo, she held the hand of an older man in bed, who appeared to be dying. He was amazed. Before age forty or so, Sally had already done much more for people than most do for others by the age of eighty. As he continued to explore, he knew he was in spiritual space—space that moved with Mrs. O'Hara.

As he progressed to the far wall, more photos showed that she had worked in the coal towns of West Virginia, the disease-drenched country of Haiti and famine-stricken Ethiopia. She and her husband worked with inner-city rape victims, among others. He sensed joy, despite the anguishing scenes he viewed, because of the sacrificial work Sally did for others. A fleeting moment brought him back to the days that he spent looking for the cases that no one wanted and those in which he made a difference in the lives of others less fortunate. He remembered the fulfillment of fighting for those where justice seemed to be absent.

Clifton wanted to take a look at more pictures, but he saw that Sally seemed uncomfortable with the attention he was giving her. He asked if they could go back to the living room for another cup of tea. She nodded, and in silence they walked back and sat as before.

With a smile Clifton hadn't seen that day, Sally said, "I was pleased that I observed you looking at the faces of my past and didn't rummage through the plaques, gifts and such that engulf that room. *You looked at the people.*"

Trying to paste the entire experience together, Clifton was confused, thinking it might be best to talk directly about what he was thinking.

"Look, I, like you, Mrs. O'Hara, fashion myself to be blunt and to the point, but it is difficult for me to say what I'm thinking."

"Well, go ahead, spit it out. I've heard a few things in my day that would make a linebacker blush."

"Mrs. O'Hara, you did all these things for so many and you are now alone. I mean you are dying and it looks like to me that you are dying alone—by yourself. That saddens me."

Pretending to be serious, Sally lowered her eyebrows. "Oh, hell. I think I called on the wrong neighbor," she said with a hearty laughter. "No, my dear. Look around. Do you think I am, if truth be told, alone?"

Clifton felt she missed his point. He was genuinely tormented at the fact that she was alone and that she had called him, a perfect stranger, to help her.

"What I mean is that your husband is gone, there are no children or family to speak of, and even your neighbors think of you as a crazy woman who does little for anyone." At that moment, Clifton knew he stepped over the line and was being disrespectful. He knew that she wasn't that person that the neighbors gossiped about. "Oh, I apologize. That's not what I meant… but it seems evident that you have no one because you called on me. I'm someone you don't know. Don't you feel alone in your time of genuine need?" Clifton said, at once slinking back in his chair.

With quiet restraint, Sally said, "heavens no, but you do present your case with logic and you do so with verve. But with any additional information, your case goes south. Believe m, I understand what you are saying. Let me tell you some things."

Frustrated, Mrs. O' Hare got up, slowly walked over to a bay window, pulled back the sheers and gazed out. She took a few deep breaths, and then looked back to Clifton, shaking her head.

She paused another moment and began to speak in a peaceful and affecting manner. "Compassion, you see, is in my soul and I am fortunate for this. Just like you, I suspect, I approach every person I meet with openness. No matter if I'm in Africa or in some city in this country. I am open to others and put them in the center of my attention. This way I can communicate and enjoy meaningful relationships with them. It's rather simple, don't you see? If we don't help each other, what good are we? Compassion is universal."

Poker-faced, Clifton sat up and listened.

"Because I wanted to be open to them, it made no difference about how they responded to me. I am responsible for my own actions, as well as my own happiness and sense of self worth. No one gives that to me. The government doesn't do this for me, my priest doesn't do this for me, and my political party certainly doesn't do this for me. *I do this for me.* If you want others to respond to you in a positive way, you must first respond to them in an open and positive manner... but then again it's more than that."

Clifton was struck by her emotion and sense of grounding. He felt like he was naked, stripped of the shield of his Brooks Brother suit. He had told himself to reserve judgment, stop and listen... but he hadn't until now.

As if talking to a child, he said in a fatherly tone, "I follow you... but you are alone right now and you will still be alone when the first snow comes. You *are* by yourself."

Her eyes welled up. "I am with *you*, am I not?"

"Why yes, but..."

Before he could finish his thought, Sally interrupted, saying with conviction, "Everyone wants to be happy, Clifton. All people, no matter who they are, want to avoid suffering. They want a chance to live life to its fullest with good physical, mental and spiritual health. That's about it—it's humanity's song. No one on this planet has more of a right to be this way than anyone else. This is what Mr. O'Hare and I have done for years. We have tried to alleviate suffering and at the same time value each person for who they were and not for whom we hoped they were. I gained a kinship and a commonality with those I met. I gained so much more from them than they did from me. I hold each one close to my heart. I am full up, Mr. Haywood. I'm full up! I don't give a rat's you-know-what if you don't believe me."

Clifton was absolutely stunned by her discourse. He knew she was right. He knew that her life was full. He had a flashback to his youth and the values he learned from his hardworking parents. He remembered how his father spoke of compassion—he saw very little of it anymore in his daily life.

The moment froze. A second before all would become totally uncomfortable, Sally continued. "I feel something. Maybe it's the souls of everyone I met and even those I wished I'd met. We're all in this thing together. No sir, I am not alone and will not be alone for as long as I live, and then some. Do you now understand what I am all about?"

"Yes, I do understand. And if you excuse my saying so, I think you had to kick my you- know-what for me to get it." Clifton did not completely *get it* but he was near that point of realization and tasted it; he needed more time after spending a great deal headed in another direction. Kindly, he thought of her and what she needed. He thought it was best to move forward with the reason he was summoned by her.

Sally walked across the room to the entrance of a sunroom. Clifton was being gracious, but worried that Sally might see through him. In due time, he knew he would understand her. *He wanted to.* The room was bright and comfortable, although the sun was at eye level, making his vision uncomfortable. A variety of exotic plants thrived against a backdrop of pines, oaks and evergreens in the yard.

Sally took a seat in a small, white wicker chair. Clifton followed, sitting directly across from her in an identical wicker chair. This time he was more at ease. He gazed outside at the beautiful trees and their colorful leaves, ready to drop from each bony twig. Her garden was a bit overgrown and contrasted with her manicured front yard that the neighbors could see. Squirrels and rabbits played there, even as dusk settled in.

It was a significant moment for Clifton, as he was accustomed to black and white corporate offices at this time of day, followed by the gray, blurring drive of the freeway to his home. He realized that so much is before him. So much eluded him.

"You can help me before that snow comes. I will not be alone."

Sally told Clifton that she wanted her estate and everything in it sold and given anonymously to the four charities that she and her husband worked with for over half a century. She asked him to cremate her remains and bring her ashes back to her birthplace, a mountain in Virginia and, alone, let them flutter in the breeze to settle where they might. She asked for him to say a prayer, not for her, but for those she left behind, asking God to help his servants learn to be open to their fellow man, and feel in their hearts what she felt in hers—compassion. This was her song and she hoped it would not fade when she was reborn.

Latent as it had become, a feeling of empathy washed his soul. Sally was hope.

Clifton finally got it. After all, Cliff was a good man.

———— ∞ ————

I never look at the masses as my responsibility; I look at the individual. I can only love one person at a time—just one, one, one. So you begin. I begin—I picked up one person. Maybe if I didn't pick up that one person, I wouldn't have picked up forty-two thousand.... The same thing in your church, your community. Just begin—one, one, one.

— Mother Teresa

How far you go in life depends on your being tender with the young, compassionate with the aged, sympathetic with the striving, and tolerant of the weak and strong. Because someday you will have been all of these.

— George Washington Carver

In the end is my beginning.

— T.S. Eliot

———— ∞ ————

All people want freedom from suffering. They want happiness. Some of these people we know but most we do not. Foe or friend, this essence we all possess is identical in each of us. Our sameness makes us human as it is a thread linking our best with our worst. It's all there in everyone of us.

We learn to be compassionate when we allow our needs, feelings and thoughts to be replaced with those of others—strangers too. Compassion is a responsibility and it takes a personal commitment to peel back our egos, our sometimes naïve, and at times ugly, veneer.

FLUB UPS AND FUTURE WISHES

In eternity there is indeed something true and sublime.
But all these times and places and occasions are now and
here. God himself culminates in the present moment, and
will never be more divine in the lapse of all the ages.
                                        – Henry David Thoreau

One today is worth two tomorrows.
                                        – Benjamin Franklin

The jagged edge of the wind penetrated his trench coat as Eric briskly trotted from the parking deck, head down, to the building. A tall, lean man with a pleasant face and matching disposition, Eric wiped the cold mist from his mustache with the back of his hand and combed his fingers through his brown- and gray-tinged bangs as the revolving door gained momentum and deposited him into the pinkish and terracotta toned marble atrium.

Sliding more than usual on the slick veneer floor, he paused, cautiously approaching each step with an inherent measured temper. Like a wallop, the aroma from *Joe's Joe*, a perennial favorite of the newspaper employees, hit Eric's nostrils, tempting him to stop for a cup of coffee. As usual, he resisted, instead proceeding across the vestibule towards the elevator.

He peered up at the huge hands of the atrium's art deco clock, wondering if time would get the best of him. Not today, he thought. Picking up his pace, he passed the guard seated behind the information desk, and, as they did everyday, exchanged smiles and a nod. Eric pressed the elevator button.

While keeping his eyes fixed above the elevator doors at the lighted numbers, behind him approached his supervisor, Ollie Burdone. Ollie was as robust as his ego, and when he smiled, his teeth were well hidden as his cheeks swelled. He was the only man Eric knew who would perspire in a howling nor'easter in February.

"Mornin', Eric. Got the contracts from Way-Mart to bed yet?"

"Hey Ollie, cold day isn't it? Ah, no. Not yet. I just got the deal yesterday at about four so I'm still working on it. Not to worry, it's coming."

"Sounds good. Just be sure to stay on top of it. We need this commission big-time," he sputtered anxiously. "Alright then, I'm gonna grab a cup. See you later."

Eric walked onto the empty elevator as Ollie turned and sauntered towards the coffee shop.

Riding nonstop to his floor, the elevator doors opened and Eric walked down the lifeless, fluorescent-lighted hall, rounded a corner, and in through oversized double glass doors to his office. As he did every day, with the same urgency and ritualistic manner, he hung up his coat on the rack by his door, turned on his desk lamp and radio, and before sitting, walked down the hall to a tiny windowless room to make a pot of coffee.

He was always the first to arrive. Eric relished the time to sip his coffee in quiet, answer emails without interruption, and getting a jump on his day. His hands still numb from his commute, he rubbed them together as he waited for the steady dribble of Colombian Supreme.

He had embarked on, and would endure through, and end his day, like all others.

Eric had tolerated a daily commute of thirty-two congested miles round-trip from home to downtown for more than thirteen years. He slogged five days a week, hoping to stumble upon a little variety, and pulled down a modest salary that grew at the pace of a melting glacier. As a mid-level executive for the city's newspaper, he hoped his craft and dreams would lead to greater possibilities. What those possibilities might be, Eric worried he'd never know.

Earlier in his career, he had spent time placing phone calls to sell the benefits of advertising to local businesses. The circulation of the paper was close to one million readers, and his potential client list was long. Canvassing and cold-calling businesses resulted in immediate sales, but the usual upshot was a lengthy string of rejections. It ebbed and flowed, but mostly ebbed.

Employed and trained by the newspaper since graduating college, he had gained competence and managed sustained streams of steady successes for most of his years there. Hardworking, his dedication rivaled that of a faithful hound. But the advent of the internet and explosion of niche marketing stepped ahead of traditional media, and the established and conventional advertising procedures had all but been rendered obsolete. Cutbacks were inevitably the result. His allegiance, though, paid off when he was "saved" from a downsizing period in the late nineties.

The newspaper rebounded with strategic planning and the implementation of digital technology. As Eric's fortune had it, he was offered a ten-percent increase to manage the restructured and expanded advertising and accounts department. But after only two years in his new role, Eric had grown weary of staff issues and could not understand why others weren't as diligent as he when drilling deeper for business. Turnover was overwhelming. Feeling burned out and disillusioned, he kept his feelings neatly concealed and went about what he needed to do to get by. "The clothes dryer is broken," "Paying for the braces will set us back": these phrases rang in his head with unparalleled persistence.

As with most drives home, Eric's practical, mid-size sedan meandered through interstate traffic and his mind, as usual, wandered. He thought about his car: boring, aging, and taking half the trip home before the heater blew out enough warm air to conquer the chill. He thought about his radio: almost always on the blink, and his favorite cassette tapes beginning to be more difficult to replace. Most of all, he thought about his life.

Dangerously, his focus was not on the cold, unyielding pavement below. The whisking cars, SUVs and eighteen-wheelers that sped by to either side of him were vague and sketchy images, deceptively luring him away from the reality of the soaring steel that could categorically make in impact if one would stray out of lane. Eric somehow found that he would slip into autopilot as his thoughts churned through his mind. With his head usually aching, and his stomach grumbling, he powered down the road, paying no attention to the very moment in which he was living. He was disturbed that he could drive a mile and have no recollection of what he saw and what he passed along the way.

That night, as with most nights, a series of seemingly arbitrary thoughts flickered in his consciousness. He found himself thinking of how he screwed up something with his kids the day before, and how he would make it up to them in the future. He found himself thinking that if only he studied harder in college or majored in something else—better yet, if he'd only gone to law school, his life would be a major cut above.

"Not that my life is that bad," he thought as be combated his negative reasoning. He believed his negative outlook was a nasty scar that would never go away. It was difficult for him to keep his mind focused on the positive notions as his mind raced back and forth, one moment thinking he was trapped in his own life, and the next acknowledging that he was just fine.

———

Eric, his wife Margo, and their three children, lived in Castle Summit subdivision, where they were one of the first owners sixteen years earlier. Most of the original neighbors were gone or moved away. Some took other jobs, allowing them to upgrade to a newer subdivision, while others left the area altogether. With this exodus went many of Eric and Margo's closest friends. While others moved on to new, exciting experiences, they remained: stable and simple.

Soon after, Margo left her full-time job as a nurse to be at home with their children, and since Eric's annual increases were marginal, their current house would have to suffice. Each day was fresh, and each moment was gratifying for Margo. She focused moment-by-moment as she took care of their children. They had sacrificed some pleasures and possessions, but it was worth it to Margo and, Eric agreed, it would be a priceless gift to his children. Eric, however, felt disconnected.

———

During his commute was the best time for Eric to think through the clutter in his brain. He would dream.

"I'd love to love my day like Margo loves her day," he would think.

"When will that happen for me?"

When opportunities arose, Eric knew he could recognize those break, and everything for him would be great.

"I'm ready for it. It's gonna happen to me—it really is."

When these thoughts flowed through his brain, he would find himself feeling a natural high—a warm tingle throughout his body as a smile enveloped his face. He'd pop in one of his favorite eighties tapes and crank the volume of his car stereo.

"Ah, here it is… the theme from *St. Elmo's Fire*."

And for those fleeting moments, everything was all right in Eric's world..

Every Friday at quitting time, Eric had gotten into the habit of stopping off at an exit about halfway home at a local micro-brewery and restaurant called Fillmore's. Fillmore's was a new account of his, a trendy place heralding superb reviews. There, on Friday afternoons, was the *Fry 'em Up Friday's* promotion, complete with half-priced fried appetizers and a trio of jazz musicians called Fryer Tuck's. It had been an overwhelming success, helping many of the patrons make the transition from work week to weekend that much smoother.

Once inside the doors, Fillmore's paid homage to President Fillmore, touting that they were the only business in the country that honored and revered the esoteric U.S. President. Under a large reproduction of the late President was an inscription that read: "A President with little to his credit, but one who seized a moment in history."

The bar was the focal point. It was ornate and made of dark mahogany, surrounded by high, plush stools. The place was adorned with paneling to match the bar, and indirect lighting that illuminated only what they wanted their customers to see. A large window opened to one side of the bar, allowing all to witness how their beer was brewed.

Eric thought that stopping in was good business. He was offered free appetizers since he handled the account. Halfway during his first visit, he decided that he liked being there. He thought he could become a regular. After about the third time, he would find his barstool, loosen his tie, turn off his cell phone, plant his elbows on the bar and order a Sam Adams. He likened the place to the television show *Cheers*, but didn't see himself as any of the fixtures on that or any other sitcom. He didn't think he was *that* pathetic. One beer alone in a crowded tavern, he would muse, isn't *really* drinking alone—especially since he made a point to talk to a few folks.

After a few weeks, Eric could honestly report back to Margo that he, indeed, was not drinking by his lonesome. The night before, Eric had overheard bits and pieces of a conversation of an older gentleman playfully teasing one of the waitresses. A tall, young lady, a third his age, she knew him by name, and when they talked, each sentence was punctuated with laughter. As she turned from him, her long blonde hair whipped around her back and she gave him a wink. A moment later, Eric couldn't help but observe scores of patrons who stopped by to speak to this man. Most left him with a smile.

Eric caught the attention of the waitress. When she approached him he quietly asked, "Who is that man at the end of the bar?"

"Why, that's Griff Franklin. He's here a lot. I'd say he's a regular," she smiled. She turned and sashayed behind the bar.

Not giving it much thought, Eric drank what remained in his glass, paid his tab and as he walked by Griff, he gave him a friendly nod. Griff returned the nod with a simple question.

"Join me?"

Eric was caught off-guard, but sincerely flattered. He casually nodded, sitting down on the bar stool next to Griff.

"My name is Griff."

"You can call me Eric."

Eric found out that Griff had a path home similar to his own, coming from the financial district on the other side of downtown. He was thin and tall, though it was rare that Eric actually saw him standing. He had a cue-ball head, with large-framed glasses covering a rather worn atlas of a face.

For some unknown reason, he had warmed to Eric. Eric was surprised; this was a new experience for him. Eric sat tall when he was in the company of Griff. From the moment he first introduced himself to Eric, they became inseparable from the time they set foot in Fillmore's until Eric left. No matter what time Eric would end up at the micro-brewery, Griff was already there with the house specialty, a Millard, in hand, ready to order another. Even if Eric arrived unusually early, Griff was there.

As time went on, Eric gleefully anticipated and grew to look forward to their weekly meeting at Fillmore's. That moment completed his week. No matter what else went on that week, the camaraderie that emanated from this moment became extraordinarily important to him.

While Eric appreciated and enjoyed these meetings, Griff benefited from them more than Eric knew. Griff's wife of twenty-two years had passed away ten years before. They had two children, Michael and Ryan, both whom lived on the other side of the country. Griff was now a financial consultant, but this was his second career. He was once a teacher, and he, Patricia and their boys, spent a number of years abroad. Patricia was a medical doctor and Griff, who learned to teach in the seminary, taught a variety of subjects to hundreds of children over the years. After Patricia's death and continuing battles with a variety of physical ailments, Griff had given up his ministry for a new perspective in a completely different field—a new beginning.

Somewhere down the line, Eric and Griff began to call their gatherings "bull sessions". They talked about sports, their golf games and jazz. They talked about "guy" things, as Eric put it when he happily reported back to Margo about Griff. Griff had a unique perspective, coming from an older generation and a unique bent on life. At times, Eric felt that Griff's thoughts were from a distant time and place. Eric was the happiest when he and Griff raised a few golden beverages together and conducted a 'session.'

After about six months of 'sessions', Griff turned the tables on Eric. "Why," Griff asked, "do you feel so beholden to your past that you will never see again?"

Without waiting for an answer he continued, "You do something else, Eric. You mostly forsake today for a starry-eyed future." Griff's brow furrowed as he shook his head in disappointment. He continued and said, "Look, we have a great time talking here and all, but I have to be honest: it's troublesome to me. Why on earth do you do this?" His question mark was emphasized by his taking an extra large gulp of beer.

Eric sat up like someone had dropped an ice cube down the back of his shirt. He found himself scratching his head, shaken and unable to answer Griff's rather bold questions. No answer came to his mind. He didn't know where this notion came from, and he didn't quite know what he meant. He felt defensive. He felt judged.

"I knew this was too good to be true," Eric reactively thought of his friendship with Griff.

Eric felt spent and his heart raced. He took a moment and then responded.

"Isn't that what people discuss?" Eric said, agitated. "You know, Griff, people talk about what they've experienced and what they hope for in the future. Aren't we supposed to talk about our dreams and aspirations?"

With each question, Eric felt the blood leaving his face, his heart pounding so much that he felt it would work its way out of his chest.

He went on, "Don't people talk about what they did and didn't do, and the choices they made along the way?" Slowing his speech, Eric sat back and looked down. "I always thought that if you can see where you want to be one day, that it's going to happen."

"Eric, you are talking about a future that will never come. Hell, you can't even look me in the eyes. I'm sorry Eric, it's hard for me to tell you this but someone has to," Griff said with a firm, yet comforting tone. "You talk about what you did and didn't do. That stuff is over and will never happen again. It's not real. Do you hear me?"

Eric's hands began to feel clammy. A nerve in his neck began to twitch and his mouth went dry. He took a small sip of beer and with a cracking voice he asked, "What are you talking about Griff?"

Griff, like an anchorman on the eleven o'clock news, emotionless and still, explained, "Don't you see? We've talked about many things over the months, but I'm afraid our conversations always center around one thing: your past flub ups and your future wishes. The future you are talking about will never come, buddy. The question is: how do you live now—today?"

Eric's head throbbed and he felt listless. Griff started back like a charging bull.

"You dismiss where you are right now. You always do. You talk about the future so much that you miss the beauty staring you in the face, and that's not my sorry old mug—it's the here and now," Griff said, pausing for a swig from his glass.

Eric began to speak, but Griff interrupted, "Today and this very moment are *most* important. See, the past is over and doesn't exist anymore, and the future will never get here. This second, the present is the only time that exists. When you get to that "future" moment, it is on top of you, get my drift? You keep looking ahead, but each moment is tied to the next. Live each moment to the fullest and what comes from it will prove to bring you happiness."

Eric never heard Griff string so many abstract thoughts together and wasn't sure he liked it. "What happened to our conversations about the Steelers?" he lamented.

Eric again felt a rush of emotions come from the bottom of his stomach and blurted out, "This is totally against my thinking. I mean, I have goals and, once I get there, it will be time to celebrate. What I'm doing now is just the precursor to what will be better times for me. Anyway, every second of every day seems so ordinary, so empty. Life must be better than what I see every day."

Puzzled, Griff looked him in the eyes. He took in a long breath.

"Eric, your journey is just as vital as where you think you want to be. Life is just that. We are meant to live it all, not just a few select points along the way. The ride is to be enjoyed or the final destination is hollow."

With that, Griff stood up and said no more. With beer left in his glass, he gently placed it on the bar. He loosened his tie and walked out the door.

"Wow," Eric thought. He calmed down, pondered what Griff told him, finished his beer and stood up, brushing the crumbs from his shirt as if he was dusting himself off from being thrown from a bronco. He paid the bartender and went home.

———— ✕ ————

The following week, Eric arrived at Fillmore's and Griff was nowhere to be seen. No funny stories. No sports conversations. No smiling waitresses.

Eric sat on the same stool as usual and waited. A stranger sat on "Griff's stool". Eric slid over to another stool insuring space for his friend. Impatient, he asked Jimmy, the bartender, if he had seen Griff. Jimmy, a large man in his late twenties with long hair pulled back in a ponytail, found a note he had tucked away in the register, slid it across the bar, and curtly walked away. After a few paces, Jimmy turned and heaved with contempt, "You *can* read?"

Eric faintly smiled and looked down. The note was in an unmarked envelope. His hands trembled as he ripped the envelope's flap, almost tearing the note. With his fingers moving in all directions as if he was working origami, he unfolded the page and read the brief message: "When you take each second of your life, and live it with fullness, and recognize the value of your journey, we will meet again."

Eric felt as if his gut had been turned inside out. He paused, composing himself. Again he read through the note, dissecting its meaning with a calmer head, "When I take each second of MY life, and LIVE it to the fullest, and I recognize the VALUE of MY JOURNEY, we will meet again."

"Wait, I've heard that my whole life." Eric thought. "Isn't that what Margo does? It's got to be true. What have I been waiting for?"

Eric digested Griff's thoughts with each deliberate sip of beer. He relished each mouthful of the lager as if it were something he never tasted before. The crackle of the carbonation glided over his tongue. He heard his own swallows. He felt the warmth of his breath on his hand that supported his chin. The music seemed to be playing louder, more rhythmic, more melodic in the background. He recognized the lyrics for once. He could smell the trail mix next to his glass. He felt the skin of his fingertips as he again touched the paper. Looking at his beer, he watched the bubbles zipping up from the bottom of his glass. Eric heard others laughing.

He began to feel something deep beneath his rib cage, and it was pleasing. With a sense of hope and courage he never felt before, he thought that he would see Griff, again, and soon.

———— ⟨⟨⟩⟩ ————

I can feel guilty about the past, apprehensive about the future, but only in the present can I act. The ability to be in the present moment is a major component of mental wellness.

— Abraham Maslow

We all want progress, but if you're on the wrong road, progress means doing an about –turn and walking back to the right road; in that case, the man who turns back soon- est is the most progressive.

— C.S. Lewis

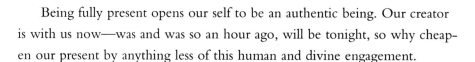

Being fully present opens our self to be an authentic being. Our creator is with us now—was and was so an hour ago, will be tonight, so why cheap- en our present by anything less of this human and divine engagement.

We have all experienced times when friends are tuned out and are not listening when we speak. We see it in their eyes. What a pitiful loss. That time will never come again, and that human connection suffers. But we may always reverse ourselves, as we are given that chance until the day we die. Living in the present is its own beauty.

GRACE

I am a part of all that I have met.
                              – Alfred, Lord Tennyson

*We make a living by what we get. We make a life by
what we give.*
                              – Winston Churchill

*How wonderful it is that nobody need wait a single minute
before starting to improve the world.*
                              – Anne Frank

Sherm always looked good in a navy blazer with gold buttons over a white, oxford cloth button-down shirt. His necktie was usually silk, with stripes, tied in a half-Windsor — always quite tight. His look was rounded off with cuffed khaki slacks and tassel-topped loafers; pretty much the uniform of the fundraising trade. Sherm was a fit, middle-aged man sporting a full frock of wavy brown hair with enough gray at his temples to lend him an air of distinction.

Like many at his stage of life, Sherm often found himself reflecting upon his place in the world, the wisdom of his decisions and the uncertain path that lay ahead. He revisited, with frequency, the early tutelage of his first boss, Leland, on what *not* to do in life. Conversely, he occasionally replayed particular events and relationships that guided him on what *to* do.

He made efforts continuously to amend the manner in which he conducted his professional life and, more importantly, reshape the very focus of his personal life.

For the first half of his fundraising career, Sherman Granger's mantra was *have gift, will travel.*

"You've got to make it happen. You'll raise more money if you ask, ask and *ask some more*," Leland would drill. "Maybe this isn't the field for you, Sherm. It's about raising money."

Leland had a much different background than Sherm, starting his career a decade earlier than he in sales, and selling his way into educational philanthropy work. For the balance of his career, Leland asserted that well-intentioned academics needed a great deal of help from someone like him. After all, Leland knew how to negotiate a deal, pulling out all the stops, bordering on the questionable. Unwittingly, young Sherman felt the wear of those words like a gnawing piranha for much of his early career, and struggled with a view of the field that was murky at best. "Am I really contributing anything *good* to this world?" Sherm would ask himself. In his early days, that thought had nearly driven him from the field.

But Sherm always knew his vocation was noble. During the tirades of his early boss, Sherm tried to remind himself that raising money served to better the students and school, giving them opportunities for growth—philanthropy, after all, is the love of mankind. "What could be nobler than being an agent of positive change and elevating what's good about humanity?" Sherm would ponder.

However, as his early career progressed, more of Sherm's time had become consumed by other aspects of the field. Among them was its loss of direction. As in any profession, his mind clouded with the ringing and annoying tone emanating from his bosses, barking the import that the bottom line dictated every move. But raising more money just to raise more money seemed to be a national trend, trickling down from universities that had the most and wanted more. After reading articles about billion-dollar campaigns, Sherm had begun to think that the soul of the vocation may be misplaced. "Those Ivies certainly know what they're doing, so it must be the right thing to do," Sherm would tell himself. His convictions flopped like a tuna pulled on deck by a fisherman's net. He had reached a critical juncture in his career, and was immersed in doubt.

Grace entered his life at the right time.

Sherm, now the head of a growing department of fundraising officers, needed a new assistant director. His former assistant garnered an abundance of experience over the past five years, as Sherm gave him a stake in the program. Sherm's new appointment was petite, with an easy smile and green eyes that sparkled. Janice had many of the attributes that Sherm wanted in a fundraiser: she knew how to listen to people and respond intelligently, she was a planner and she showed herself to be a creative person, excelling in all her projects. She could talk to a wide variety of people and, best of all, she knew nothing about money, and confessed that she didn't even like it. She was perfect for the job.

At the beginning of her second week as assistant director, Sherm called Janice into his office. With an open palm, he asked her to have a seat. He moved away from his desk and sat on a small couch facing her. His office was spacious, with high ceilings, crown molding and large windows opening out to a lush green quad. In the distance was a grove of trees. Without a cloud in the sky, the sun poured into the room. It was a clear, warm day. He liked the view, watching students talk, study and play. He often found himself gazing out the window for long periods of time, thinking of the lives he touched without them even remotely knowing.

"Janice, there are a few things I want to talk to you about regarding the raising of money." Sherm started with questions. "Who has wealth? What do they think of our college? How can we get to them?"

He paused and answered his own question, "You've got to identify prospects, determine their wealth, and develop strategies and maneuvers to move those prospects closer to wanting to make a substantial gift to an institution like ours. This is what experts say. What I want you to remember is something a bit different: develop real relationships. It's very simple."

"So, are you saying that what we do is more than sending letters or asking repeatedly like that guy you used to work for?" Janice said with a wry smile only she could get a way with as she remembered Sherm's infrequent but poignant laments about a time a decade and a half ago.

With a hearty laughter, Sherm continued. "Well, yes—much more."

Sherm paused, glanced at the plaques hanging on his wall and then at a photo of Grace. He turned to Janice. "Somewhere in all this *betterment of humankind*, something can be, and oftentimes is, lost. Values may be set aside, and for me, it took an introduction to Grace to find out what I already knew. Let me start another way."

Sherm took a deep breath, paused, and shared his story.

———

A few years back, when the air had cooled, and football season was well underway, Sherm had received a call from a Mr. Mercer. Mr. Mercer lived in the Shenandoah Valley, roughly one hundred miles west of his quiet cul-de-sac outside the city. He told Sherm that he was interested in making a gift to the school, and hoped that Sherm would visit his home.

"I saw your name on something that was sent to the house so I'm calling you. I hope you're the right person to talk to. It's a real pain in the butt once you get on the phone at a university. You never know who you're going to talk to and if they really care any way," Mr. Mercer said in a gruff, raspy voice.

The phone conversation was short. Sherm tried to extend it a bit by asking him leading questions, but that quickly became fruitless.

Later, upon looking up Mr. Mercer's record in the university's database, Sherm found that although he was a 1944 alumnus of the school, he had never been back to a reunion. He also wasn't a previous donor, so Sherm didn't know much about him. Sherm proceeded to do some preliminary research but could not find anything that would indicate he had any wealth to speak of. Sherm called a classmate of his, whom he knew well, to see if he could find something out about Mr. Mercer. What he found out was that, in a sense, Mr. and Mrs. Mercer had all but fallen off the planet.

"Oh brother, not another two-hundred mile round trek for a measly one hundred dollar gift," Sherm thought cynically.

It didn't matter; Sherm had other donors in the area and could stop in and see them to justify the trip.

———

The morning he had scheduled to make the trip, Sherm felt rushed and unmotivated, and didn't particularly feel like making the journey. Outside it was rather cold but clear, and a subtle frost covered the lawn and shrubs, car and driveway. All in his household were still asleep in their toasty beds with only a night-light here and there to break an unusually dark morning. Sherm had awakened to the harsh sound of his alarm clock, cursing the day he made the appointment to visit with Mr. Mercer. He showered, dressed and quietly left his bedroom with innocent envy of his wife, Laura, who had another forty-five minutes before her alarm would sound. He walked down the hall and poked his head in his daughter's room, only to see her snuggled up in a cozy ball. He noticed across the hall that his son had left his video game on throughout the night, and proceeded to tiptoe across his room, finding little carpet to plant his next step, to turn it off.

It was near dawn as Sherm took the last sip of his coffee, peeked out the kitchen window, and saw the sun's fingers touching his children's swing set. It was amazing how the filtered colors of the sky could appear so vibrant when the horizon was all but hidden by suburban trappings. Grabbing his travel mug and worn briefcase, he trudged out the back door.

Pulling out of his driveway, he almost ran over a jogging neighbor. "This must be an omen," Sherm thought. With his heart thumping double-time, he was ready to pull back in the driveway, go back inside and forget the day. But after a moment to pull himself together, Sherm found himself headed out of the concentric circles of streets in the neighborhood. The morning sun slowly crept up the horizon, shining brighter on his shoulders as he pulled onto the interstate and headed west.

Once out of the tangled streets of the subdivision and onto the highway, Sherm was more at ease. It was a new day, with new possibilities. "Traveling the opposite way of my usual plod is a nice change of pace... uplifting even," Sherm concluded. With a smile on his face, he told himself that this day was going to be more of an adventure than work—for a hundred dollars it just had to be.

Once Sherm reached the mountains, he knew he was far from his daily grind in body and spirit. As he ventured onward, he found himself keenly attuned to the beauty of his surroundings. Unlike his familiar suburban landscape, the leaves on the trees were glowing yellows and burning reds. They were seductive, almost like fine wines. He turned off his cell phone, disregarded his CD's, and cranked the volume of his car stereo to sing to the songs that came at random from the local station. The complexities of work and life melted away and, if only for a fleeting time, he felt relaxed.

As he drove deeper into the valley, Sherm's surroundings appeared more untouched and pristine. Still, he couldn't help but find his mind drawn to the daily concerns of work. He thought of what might be going on back at the office. He thought about calling his assistant to see if the $250,000 proposal he had prepared for a long-time trustee was ready for his review. He thought and thought, until finally stopping to roll down his window and take in the cool, unadulterated mountain air. "Ah, work can wait for a minute," Sherm decided.

Not sure how accurate his directions were, he decided to pull off an exit and take a look at his notes one more time. As he circled down the winding exit, he spotted a small, ramshackle vegetable stand off the shoulder, manned by an elderly farmer and his equally elderly wife. "What a pair of fools," he thought. "How much money could they expect to make sitting here in hopes that someone will stop and buy from them?"

The word "VEGITABLES" was painted on a long, cracked plank at the foot of three sawhorses, holding baskets of vegetables and some fruit. The area was known for its apples. The man was moving pumpkins off his truck and, presumably, his wife was dusting off some of the produce.

Getting out of his car to walk over to the couple, Sherm noticed the pungent mixture of vegetable odors in the soft breeze. He wasn't used to that. The farmer immediately extended his calloused, worn hand. After a short greeting by both men, Sherm asked the tall, lanky farmer if he knew Mr. Mercer and, if so, he could help by giving him directions to Mr. Mercer's home. The farmer rubbed his unshaven chin and obliged him with plain and simple directions. Before Sherm could turn to head back to his car, the farmer's wife tapped him on the shoulder, and as he turned, she smiled, holding out an apple. Her smile was beautiful. Sherm smiled back to her, took the apple, and thanked her.

Second-guessing himself, Sherm decided to speak up about their sign.

"Sir, you know the word vegetable doesn't have an "i". Kindheartedly and with a low, steady voice the farmer whispered, "Yeah, and potatoes don't have eyes either." All three laughed. "Thanks... but we know that. Our daughter painted that for us 'bout twenty years ago, I reckon. Don't have the heart to change it... but you know what were selling, don't ya?"

Sherm's eyebrows pushed upward as he gave the couple a wide grin and nodded farewell. "Nice folks," he thought.

After driving another mile or two, Sherm turned at the wrangled oak tree, per the farmer's instructions, and proceeded up a very long but straight gravel driveway, kicking up a haze of dust on his way. He could barely see where he was headed. A shabby mutt howled and chased, or rather limped by, his car up the narrow and rutted path, finally giving up to plop down in his tracks and catch his breath.

As Sherm slowed, the dust finally settled, giving a view of an old, modest home. It was a log cabin, set high on brick pylons with two stone chimneys hanging to either side. The worn, tin roof hung well over the front, creating an extra large front porch. Sherm parked the car, got out and double-checked the address. Climbing the steep, rotting stairs to the front door, he anxiously looked side to side, noticing that nothing was around other than a barn and a few other farm buildings. No neighbors.

The property was outlined by the Alleghany Mountains to one side and the Blue Ridge on the other. The horizon was miles off and the panoramic views were spectacular. Off to one side was a stream. The air was so still that Sherm heard the water rushing over large, smooth stones. "Geez, what a lonely place—but pretty."

Before he could knock on the monstrous black door, it opened, revealing a short, round man with a full head of silver hair.

"Oh, I see Mr. Fred has already greeted you," Mr. Mercer said with a broad smile.

Assuming that was the old dog, Sherm acknowledged with a subtle nod.

"Mr. Mercer?" Sherm asked, just to make sure.

"That's right fella," Mr. Mercer said with a grin, stepping aside to invite Sherm in.

Once inside, Mr. Mercer offered Sherm a comfortable chair and a mug of hot coffee, as he assumed all good folks do. What followed was a certain amount of unmemorable small talk, per Mr. Mercer's design. Sherm could tell that he had other things on his mind. He wanted to talk about something important. Sherm was right; Mr. Mercer wanted to talk about Grace.

"When I met Grace I knew she was special," Mr. Mercer said with a nostalgic glow. "What a beautiful lady. That was back in '43. We met at a school dance. I wasn't looking for her and she wasn't looking for me but we were looking to graduate, that's all. Well, I guess, that wasn't all."

Sherm was confused. He finished his coffee and Mr. Mercer asked him if he wanted a refill, but he declined.

Mr. Mercer continued to speak, nonstop, for nearly forty-five minutes about Grace. As he talked, Sherm couldn't help but notice a look in his eyes that seemed to give Mr. Mercer's words a more profound, intense meaning. Sherm wasn't sure why, but it did. Mr. Mercer just had a genuine sincerity about him when he spoke about Grace.

Sherm caught his mind wandering, quickly remembering his tight schedule and things to do back at the office. Although he was fascinated by his stories, Sherm shifted the conversation to the purpose of his being there—the gift.

Mr. Mercer continued, ignoring Sherm's attempt to divert the conversation. "You know we were married for near fifty-five years?" he said, raising his eyebrows high. "Everyday was a gift and everyday I received blessings for no reason. I'm the luckiest man alive. I was very undeserving of her many gifts but she gave them anyway. Oh, I wasn't a bad man, I just didn't understand her, but I knew I loved her."

Pausing for a moment and scratching his head he added, "I didn't understand her until she was gone."

At once Mr. Mercer's demeanor shifted. His eyes quickly welled up. He leaned forward and reached for a handkerchief from his back pants pocket, excusing himself from the room. The moment was awkward for both men.

Sherm inhaled a long breath and let it out slowly. He stood up and looked around the room. It was a large room, with a staircase that both descended to a lower floor and ascended to the attic. Two of the rustic walls were covered with lopsided, built-in bookcases, while the others boasted a variety of eccentric wall hangings; swords, pistols, African art and Native American artifacts were displayed with reverence. As Sherm walked over to examine the artifacts, he noticed that the wide-knotted pine planks did not creak. "Strange. I guess this place is sturdier than it looks," Sherm whispered to himself. The once-roaring fire in the oversized, stone fireplace was now merely embers, producing a subtle orange haze and smoky aroma. The end tables held countless frames of various sizes, accenting sixty years of living. "Wow, she was beautiful".

The exposed beam ceilings were high above, giving a feel of majesty in what could only be considered a modest dwelling. Large windows on all four walls looked out to the range of towering mountains, giving Sherm a constant reminder that he was somewhere special. He walked over to the hearth, picked up the bellow and attempted to bring life back to the smoldering embers. He gently placed some kindling on the charred wood and soon a small but ample fire emerged. He warmed his hands, wondering when Mr. Mercer would return.

"Ah yes—thank you for tending to the fire," Mr. Mercer said, quietly entering the room. "I appreciate your help. Let's sit again."

Mr. Mercer sat back, bent over to one side so he could touch Mr. Fred's head.

Abruptly he launched into a new conversation. "I made a lot of money. Yeah, I spent a lot of time making money," Mr. Mercer said, his broad grin returning. "In the early years, she would give much of what I made away. She gave it to well-deserving folks and children, but I was of another mindset, if you know what I mean. Nevertheless, her giving and giving used to infuriate me. Oh boy, I'd get steamed up. So you know what I did? I took the money from her. You know what she did?"

Intrigued by the conflict, Sherm leaned forward from his chair, barking, "No, what did she do? Oh... sorry."

"That's okay. I'm glad you're listening. Anyway, she began to give her time—she gave of herself. She was a resourceful person. She knew why she was here. Money and time were merely her tools—it's what she did with those tools."

Mr. Fred jumped up and began to howl at the door. Mr. Mercer walked over to the door and glanced out a small window. "Oh, Mr. Fred... false alarm."

Mr. Mercer resumed his seat, followed closely by Mr. Fred.

"This old hound was hers. She found him on the side of the road, oh, about sixteen years ago. He was suffering from exposure and she nursed him back to health. He misses her; so do I," he said. A pause followed his quiet and deliberate affirmation.

Mr. Mercer took a deep breath, resuming his thought. "She told me that I needed to love a few things—and people—that couldn't always show me love back. Grace practiced these random acts of kindness for no reason. She expected nothing in return. Nothing at all. She was kind. Her humility was second nature."

Pointing his thumb to his chest he explained, "Because of her, this old fool received blessings for no reason."

Sherm's keen interest was interrupted by a knock on the door. Mr. Fred was a moment late this time, springing to his paws and beginning to howl. The men looked at each other and chuckled.

Mr. Mercer walked to the door, opening it to reveal the elderly farmer and his wife, who Sherm met earlier in the day.

"Hey, Mr. Mercer. We knew that you had a guest, so we thought we'd bring over a basket of some of our favorites," explained the farmer. "We've got some apple butter, some corn pudding, and Jenny, here, went on home and wrapped up some biscuits she baked this morning."

Mr. Mercer looked very pleased. "Thanks, won't you join us?"

"No, we better get going. We had a good day and sold just 'bout everything so we ought to get back to clean up the stand. We always remember Grace telling us that the way of the earth is to empty what is full, and then what appears to be empty will fill up again. Y'all know I'm not as good with words as she was, but I think I got it about right. Anyway, she was so right. We're still blessed by her. See you soon Mr. Mercer," he said with a wave, slowly turning down the porch steps.

In less than three minutes, the couple had managed to bring joy not only to Mr. Mercer, but to Sherm as well. In such a short moment in time a great deal was shared—and accepted. Sherm was astonished. "I stopped by their stand earlier today, and they had so much there to sell. Do you mean to tell me that they sold all they had?" he asked with a confounded look.

"No, no. They probably sold about half so they made a little. They gave away the other half by doing just what they did here. They'll tell you that they want for nothing, even though they fell on hard times years ago. Grace was a good friend to them. Grace always said that prosperity is not about what we collect, but what we give to others. Who we become is what matters. Those folks are real successes in life. If you understand her logic and philosophy, then you'll know that its only when you become empty that you can be filled again—and with much more."

———— ∞ ————

After another hour of conversation had passed, Sherm noticed that the swirls of crimson and honey-colored clouds had begun to drape over the wistful Allegheny Mountains, notifying him that it was time to go.

Sherm smiled as he recounted the day's events. It could not have been a finer day, and he had all but forgotten that he had come to pick up a check.

Sherm told Mr. Mercer that it was time for him to move on. Mr. Mercer asked for another moment and left the room. As Sherm rose from his chair and gathered his things, Mr. Mercer returned and handed him a check. One hundred dollars. Sherm was pleased. Very pleased. He couldn't believe it but he was—pleased and happy to be so.

———— ∞ ————

In the following months, Sherm made it a point to stay in touch with Mr. Mercer, chatting occasionally about the events in their lives, and recalling Grace's amazing life and actions.

Over time, Mr. Mercer began to increase his donations. He did so because his bond with Sherm grew, and he knew his gift would be used to help a place that gave him and his wife so much.

Sherm ventured to the valley a few more times to visit. His last time was when Mr. Fred died and Mr. Mercer and he, with reverence, laid him to rest on a hill behind the house. What Sherm didn't know was that Mr. Mercer was also dying. Despite his ailment, Mr. Mercer had been constant in appearance and action. Sherm was oblivious to his friend's deterioration.

Almost five years to the day that Sherm first met Mr. Mercer, he got a phone call early one morning. Mr. Mercer had died in his sleep, surrounded by friends. Sherm attended the funeral. Hundreds were there to pay their respects. Despite Mr. Mercer's age and secluded home, the masses that attended his wake and memorial service weren't a surprise to Sherm. To him, the day was ironic and contrary to the first time he visited Mr. Mercer. That day, Sherm had assumed that few were in the old man's life and that he lived a lonely existence. How wrong he was.

At a gathering after the service, Mr. Mercer's friends told Sherm at great length and in many different ways how the Mercer's had touched their lives.

"…it was the same with Grace—folks just loved the Mercers," explained the old farmer.

Later that day, after talking with more of Mr. Mercer's friends, Sherm learned something new: Mr. Mercer had in fact been Dr. Mercer.

"They were who they were," said a friend.

Several months later, Sherm got a call from the Mercer's lawyer. Mr. Mercer had left $500,000 to Grace's alma mater in her memory. He left a personal message for Sherm, saying that whatever is left should go to his school to remember Grace as well. He added that Sherm would understand. He did.

———— ❧ ————

> *Many men go fishing all their lives without knowing that it is not fish they are after.*
> – Henry David Thoreau

> *Carry out a random act of kindness, with no expectation of reward, safe in the knowledge that one day someone might do the same for you.*
> – Princess Diana

———— ❧ ————

A full glass can take no more. Unless we empty it, the chance for more is lost. So it is with us. We are blessed for no reason when we practice grace.

As we empty ourselves giving to others we are miraculously filled with what we need. This brings clarity to our life's progression. This gives progression to our life's clarity.

———— ⨌ ————

IF TRUTH BE TOLD

It is our choices, Harry, that show what we truly are, far more than our abilities.
> – Dumbledore: Harry Potter and the
> Chamber of Secrets by J. K. Rowling

The most pathetic person in the world is someone who has sight but has no vision.
> – Helen Keller

A marriage engagement seldom begins with zirconium. Everyone wants what is true—the honest, real deal.

Likewise, when one gets something for nothing, *it is nothing*. On the surface, a veneer may seem brilliant but in time it becomes flat. Imitations are shallow, worthless… empty. With people, it's the same thing. Champion athletes, uncovered as cheats, lose face. Executives who skim profits from their clients lose trust. Those who sidestep the law lose freedom. But worst of all, those who put stock in possession loses oneself—at least that is what Glen thought.

———⚬⚬⚬———

Framing Washington D.C. and weaving in and out of the city is the worst and most confusing maze of concrete, steel and asphalt in the country. These lifeless and monotonous arteries are fed by major, colorless tributaries all linked to a mesh of streets that flow to hundreds of similar looking neighborhoods with thousands of similar looking houses. In those houses are millions of people. Because of those millions of different people, no two homes are the same, even when the floor plans are alike.

This, in a way, is where life begins.

———⌘———

Clayton and Bronwyn Dunn lived in a house in one of these neighborhoods. An acrylic white picket fence all but separated them from their neighbors—or so it seemed to them both. Their house was transitional in style with vaulted ceilings and an open floor plan. Cold tiles and hardwood covered many surfaces. For days after their maid labored throughout, the scent of polish would still linger in the air.

To some, their house epitomized the pinnacle of curb appeal. Their sculpted and manicured yard was designed by a landscape artist, the stained glass above their front door by a local artisan, and their mailbox by a custom woodworker. Their yard boasted a pronounced contrast to all others on the street.

Glen and Candace Murphy lived next door to Clayton and Bronwyn. One of the more modest houses in the neighborhood, their home was comfortable and clean. Frequently the thumping sounds of the clothes dryer rivaled that of the dishwasher, emanating fresh traces of powdered soap mixtures and dryer softening sheets throughout their home. Eclecticism due to practicality was their way.

Simple and utilitarian, the Murphys' yard was covered with an array of children's toys. Trikes, balls and a sandbox graced their backyard. Under those toys, the lawn was a mixture of crabgrass and fescue with an occasional dandelion, maintaining a good bottle green hue that most neighbors didn't seem to mind.

Life teemed in other ways at the Murphys'. Their home was in suitable shape, but upon close inspection, some flaking paint and a torn window screen would keep them from including their home in the garden week tour. Their house was frozen in the eighties, and reflected the owners' roots. It was a place of celebrated beginnings and frolics, from first steps to belly slides down the carpeted stairs.

Glen and Candace moved into the neighborhood eight years before Clayton and Bronwyn, before the real estate market exploded in suburb

Washington D.C. Even so, both Glen and Candace held dependable jobs and, with their combined earnings, they were able to manage their house payments, and even some improvements in the early days.

Soon children came: Luke, their oldest, followed by Amy and Courtney. While she sincerely enjoyed her job, Candace always wanted to be a stay-at-home mom, and while Luke was a baby, she felt the nagging financial pressure to continue teaching at the middle school. Like holding back a waterfall, the Murphys felt enormous financial pressure, continually struggling to manage the costs of a growing family and a home on only Glen's teaching salary.

Cutting costs where they could, Glen and Candace had faith that Glen's career would steadily progress. Ever since his first year of teaching, Glen's career goal was to move from the high school teaching ranks to principal—fulfilling his passion and allowing for a more comfortable life for his family.

As fate would have it, Glen received news that he was promoted to the school's assistant principal only two months before Amy was born. His hard work had paid off. With the added responsibility came a healthy pay increase. Finally, he and Candace were able to make a few financial adjustments. Candace could safely leave teaching and spend her time with her children; a time she knew would come and go before she could catch her breath, but wanted to enjoy every moment as long as it lasted.

—ɷ—

Clayton, a pharmaceutical sales rep, managed a lucrative portfolio with clients as far north as Johns Hopkins in Baltimore, and a number of major hospitals and medical centers in and around the nation's capitol. His job was functional and purposeful. Whether he enjoyed what he did was secondary, as long as he made the kind of living that left him and his family wanting for nothing.

Bronwyn met Clayton during their college days. Clayton and his fraternity brothers would drive the thirty or forty miles from their campus to visit Bronwyn's all-female school. They met at a Sunday afternoon tea dance. Bronwyn, who was never interested in studies as much as shopping malls, spent her days at school searching for that special someone who could help her achieve her goals. She found Clayton—the right man who could provide the kind of life she had come to expect.

Soon after graduation day, Clayton and Bronwyn got married and lived for a time in Georgetown, in a three-story renovated Victorian. The luster of the ancient hardwood and elaborate molding was a serious draw for Bronwyn. Just having a fireplace in most of the rooms, although all but one functioned, was a source of pleasure to them. Near Capitol Hill, they enjoyed rubbing elbows with freshman senators and other up and coming politicians. Camera-laden tourists, and parking the Benz two blocks from home, were a source of irritation for Clayton.

Once Victoria was born, they headed for the suburbs. Before much time passed, they had spent a considerable amount of money they didn't have on their house and yard. They enclosed a screen porch to keep the insects at bay, they remodeled their kitchen although they only occasionally used the microwave oven, and they knocked out walls to remodel a bathroom to create a home spa.

The yard underwent major changes as well. The landscape artist added several new mounds of earth. A putting green took shape next to a new stone patio with a gushing fountain. A fish pond teeming with large carp was carved out adjacent to the patio. On the other side of the pickets, Glen refurbished and stained their deck, built an oversized playhouse for Amy and Courtney, and built a T-Ball diamond for Luke.

While Clayton and Bronwyn bought new SUVs every two years, Glen and Candace continued to drive an old mini van, and an even older sedan, with nearly one hundred and fifty thousand miles on the odometer. Vacations were a rarity at Glen and Candace's home. When they had a chance to pick up and go, they liked to hike in the mountains or spend long weekends at the beach. Spending time at the community pool took much of their summer days.

Clayton and Bronwyn traveled throughout the year. Cancun was a favorite, as well as Vail. Sometimes they even brought along Victoria.

The couples liked one another, but socialized with others. They were "over-the-fence neighbors" and spent time talking behind the pickets. Glen and Candace enjoyed the company of others in the neighborhood for cookouts and an occasional glass of wine or beer. Clayton and Bronwyn usually spent time with those they met at the tennis club.

Conversations between Candace and Bronwyn were often a speck stilted, finding common ground only when talking about the weather, what grows well in the region and what bargains might be found at the local grocery store. When it came to discussing bargains, however, Candace felt that Bronwyn was slumming a tad just to be neighborly. As far as the men, the conversation was similarly superficial, highlighted by brief exchanges about sports, cars, and the best fertilizer for the lawn.

A touchy yet amiable steadiness emerged unwittingly as a kind of hall-mark that was comfortable for the two families. This balance was always an ounce away from the emergence of a new measurement. But like drawing a line in the sand, one cannot retreat.

—⚬⚬⚬—

One day, nature called out for attention and the Murphy's responded. It was a chilly Saturday. By all accounts, it was a gorgeous day and the sky was cobalt blue and the fiery red and golden yellow leaves drifted in slow motion end-over-end to the yards below. Puffy, white clouds took turns hiding the sun but created periodic cool breezes in the air. It was the kind of morning that all seemed fair as the intense warm rays of the sun that filtered through the limbs of the trees that held tight to the last of their leaves. The shadows rendered by the pickets that separated these families appeared a bit sharper as the pointed ends of the darkened images on the ground squeezed tightly on the grassy surface of the Murphy's yard.

Glen, a tall, thin man in his thirties had wavy sandy hair that touched his collar and covered the tops of his ears. It was seldom perfectly groomed. With a commanding presence, his deep voice resounded from his angular jar and its melody gave all who heard him a sense of reassurance. He wore old grass stained tennis shoes, olive colored hiking shorts and his faded and frayed traditional college sweatshirt as he raked the leaves in large piles in the back-yard. He was in no hurry and would gladly pause to kick a battered soccer ball with his children or to stop to talk with Candace as she swept the deck clear of last week's leaves that were curled and brown.

Pulled back in a pony tail, Candace had long chestnut hair. After three pregnancies, her wardrobe had changed somewhat, but also due to their three children she bore a sense of confidence that radiated delicate warmth, always making Glen stop and smile. Her smile too came without warning as she offered hugs to her children, declaring to herself what she was doing as at that given time. Her house reflected her attention to her family.

Clayton emerged from his house like a bear from hibernation. He was donning his latest L.L. Bean slacks and his polo shirt that wrapped around his barrel chest and was painfully tucked in his pants. He carried a tall coffee mug in his right hand and newspaper neatly tucked under his left arm. Somewhat balding, Clayton had a very pleasant face and always looked like he was in a good mood. He extended his hand that held the mug, nearly sloshing coffee on his arm as he waved to the Murphy's. He negotiated with a chaise lounge by his pond, and as he plopped into the chair a rogue and rather large drop of coffee anointed his forehead. Rubbing the back of his hand above his brow, he settled himself. He read his paper.

After some time passed, Clayton, with precision, folded his newspaper and put it on a small table to his side. With a semblance of grace, he resurrected himself from his reclined position and walked over to the fence that divided his world from theirs and motioned Glen over to chat.

As Glen approached the picket fence, Clayton, as if in mid-sentence, began.

"I've been promoted at the company and we're expanding. We're looking for more sales reps in the western part of the state and I thought of you. I'm doing the hiring. Are you interested?"

Perplexed with the question, Glen couldn't help but to raise his eyebrows, creating his rarely seen forehead lines. Thinking that his answer would discourage any more talk on the subject he said, "Thanks but I'm doing just fine at the school."

With evident confusion in his eyes, Glen continued, "You can't be serious, Glen. I mean this is a chance to make some *real* money. Some real money! You and Candace can make a better life for you and your family. You can get a new car, go on vacation… you can enjoy your life. What do you say?"

Little Amy ran up and hugged Glen's leg. Looking down to her with a smile Glen continued, "Clayton, I don't know how Candace and I could wish for a better life. She and I love and support each other, our children bring us joy every moment and we are both working doing what we cherish." He paused a moment and, sensing that Clayton wasn't listening but thinking of what he would say next, Glen calmly added, "Things can be tough sometimes and, yeah, we have some tensions about finances, but we remind ourselves, it's just money—it's *just* money."

Clayton was now very confused and with an obvious arrogance blurted, "Buddy, don't take this the wrong way but if you can't see an opportunity that is staring you in the face and being given to you, you've got to be crazy."

Keeping his emotions well hidden, Glen, ready to retort, was interrupted by Candace. From across the yard she called to him, telling him that she was going inside to make grilled cheese sandwiches and tomato soup for the family's lunch.

"Thanks honey. That'd be great—I'll have two. I'll be there in just a moment. Suddenly I feel hungry," Glen boomed to Candace and turned back to Clayton. Beginning to feel very aggravated, but knowing he did not have to justify his life decisions, he decided to give Clayton a personal history lesson.

"You know, I was accepted to Harvard for grad school when I graduated from college but turned it down. You might think that I was crazy for that too. But I thought of how I spent a number of summers working with children less fortunate than I, and I thought of a lot of things. I weighed whether or not I wanted to spend my days chasing dollars or chasing kids. Besides, I met Candace during one of those summers. It was our junior year. We both had a real desire to teach. So we decided to teach—but you know that."

Like the rainwater beading off Clayton's waxed SUV, Glen's words didn't sink in. Clayton was now perplexed with Glen's life decisions as well as his answer about the job opportunity. "Glen, I thought you were crazy but you are right. Now I *know* you are crazy."

Ignoring Clayton's behavior, Glen, in a composed manner, said, "Did you always want to sell pharmaceuticals? I mean it is a great job but was that your dream?"

Totally disarmed, Clayton blew out a puff as if he just inhaled a cigarette. "My dream? I never gave it much thought. I knew I wanted to make money for all the things that I wanted." He paused and reassuring himself he straightened his back and continued, "I want things, you know? Bronwyn *wants* things and we want Victoria to *have* things. I mean, if you can get what you want, well why not? There's nothing wrong with that. I make an honest living and the stuff I sell helps people—nothing wrong with that," Clayton said in his rambling fashion.

Shaking his head, Glen started up, "You're not going to convince me that you are selling what you're selling because it 'helps people.' I'm not buying that. It's because you want 'stuff' as you said. And to answer your question, there is nothing wrong with that. But let me ask you a few other questions: Are you being true to yourself? Do the things that you say you need control you or are you in control of those things? I mean, our possessions clutter our perspective. Our joy comes from inside, Clayton. I don't want to be preachy but I am a teacher—the only thing that separates us is *things*. This damn picket fence separates us."

Clayton paused for a moment, trying to convince himself that he had answered with great hesitation and deliberation, "Well, it's true that I like having the stuff I can buy with my paycheck. So... yes, I'm true to myself. I don't know what you mean about things cluttering our perspective...you've done a nice job cluttering mine."

Glen went on to say, "In the end, do you think you will get everything you and Bronwyn want? I mean, doesn't it get harder and harder to satisfy all your wants today and all those coming up down the road? When will you be satisfied?"

There was a long moment of silence, and then from the patio Bronwyn called over to Clayton, "Are you ready to go out to lunch?"

Clayton responded, "Yeah, in just a minute. Where's Victoria?"

"Oh, she's in her room watching TV—I think."

Glen nodded to both his neighbors, turned away and headed for his grilled cheese and tomato soup.

As he trudged to his house knowing very well that he had made no impact on Glen, he thought back to the time that his path diverged with little warning. He thought of what was emblazoned over the portal of the camp's dinning hall that summer he worked in New Hampshire:

"Thwart the cold wind of deceit; know the warmth
of truth—it draws one nigh."
"Huh... then again, perhaps not everyone wants what is true."
Some seek something else. They seek zirconium.

---

*For what will it profit a man if he gains the whole world,
and looses his own soul? Or what will a man give in
exchange for his soul?*
　　　　　　　　　　　－ Jesus, The Bible; Mark 8:36-37

Thank God for the things that I do not own.
　　　　　　　　　　　－ St. Teresa of Avila

All that is gold does not glitter...
　　　　　　　　　　　－ J.R.R. Tolkien

What we own cannot reflect who we are, for what can be owned, can be sold. Things that soon become outdated, that break, and those in which we lose interest, are easily obtained and easily discarded. As we accumulate, we lose sight of so much; but how could that be? We may become blinded by what our ego yearns for, and the weight of what we own may become suffocating. Pause, reflect, release and renew.

OLD MAN SINCLAIR

Experience is not what happens to you; it is what you do with what happens to you.

— Aldous Huxley

To myself I am only a child playing on the beach, while vast oceans of truth lie undiscovered before me.

— Sir Isaac Newton

Driving home with his windows tightly fused to the window frame, Ted's path home from work was predominantly that of a fresh asphalt surface, cold and stagnant. Upon his occasional glance from side to side, he would typically lament the fact that few trees remained in the concrete surroundings, victims of newly built shopping malls, car dealerships and other franchises. "Just what we need," he would think. Just today he had noticed that sod was being readied to be laid, wound in huge circles like wagon wheels, soon to be rolled out, and pieced together like a jigsaw puzzle to decorate a row of plainly designed cinder block and faux-front businesses. "Gosh, no matter how they dress up concrete blocks, they're still ugly...."

Something, however, struck a chord inside him as he drove home as the sun slowly lost its intensity in the western sky. He was ecstatic to be headed home; this week had stretched extra long at the office due to glitches and problems that now seemed meaningless in the scheme of his life.

Once he had driven clearly away from the stink of the unnatural, Ted rolled down the windows, allowing the cool fragrant air to tousle his dark, middle-aged hair and muffle the music from his static-laden car radio, urging him to crank the volume and sing even louder. Gliding down the crowned streets, Ted looked around at the neighborhood, noticing that the stingiest of trees had finally agreed to give the world their buds. Many were popping. It was a moment meant to be memorized.

Suddenly, Ted was amazed at what a scent could trigger. A gleaming, redolent feeling enveloped him that was less of a surprise, but one that he was unwittingly, but calmly, looking for. "Everyone should experience such smells at some time in their lives," he thought.

Ted's neighborhood had been built nearly twenty years earlier by a developer who had tagged four times more trees to leave standing than was typical, giving today's community a desirable reputation of established wooded lots. Windows down and approaching his home, Ted knew it was springtime, as a whip of pungent air took him by surprise like a smack from a misinformed girlfriend. He took a heaping whiff of the unmistakable aroma—freshly cut grass. "Can't appreciate the full effect in the city; not at all. Not in the country either—far too much competition. There's only one place on earth to fully appreciate the pleasure of this certain smell. Ah, suburbia."

Kirsten, Ted's wife of twenty years, just off her knees from planting chrysanthemums in her island garden, was adjusting the sprinkler heads to water the yard. Tall and slim, she was equally self-effacing and plain speaking. Her coarse, auburn hair had a hint of gray, and was cropped close to her head, outlining her clear, soft face.

Ted swept into the driveway, flung open the car door and, leaving it that way, playfully rushed up to his wife and wrapped his arms around her soil-covered torso. "The bouquet is best right here—really." Ted, in his usual bombastic fashion continued his soliloquy, "my dear, the rationale is quite simple. Here, there are so many lawns cared for and fussed over by so many compulsive homeowners, who are all striving for the greenest, thickest and weed-free quarter-acre real estate this side of any downtown."

"Ted, I'm so glad you're happy to see me," Kirsten said laughing. "Even though I haven't a clue as to what brought this on."

This was nothing new. Ted was the same man she met two decades ago, and with age, when most men lose their youthful quirkiness and move to their rightful place as curmudgeons, Ted was different. He hadn't changed one bit. She let him have his original moments, especially when it came to his wacky obsession with the nuances found in nature, like freshly cut grass, that most people overlook.

"Think of it... on any given Saturday, like tomorrow, on a street this size you can hear up to five mowers going at once. I'm talking blade-on-blade cutting and shredding all at once. What a delight!"

"You're asking for it. No more talk of grass... I'm busy here. Go on inside," Kirsten giggled. With that, Ted turned and walked up the eight stairs to the front porch and deposited himself, spread-eagled, on the porch swing.

Kirsten spontaneously erupted in laughter, wiping a drop of perspiration from her cheek, leaving a smudge of yard on her face. Shaking her head at Ted, she walked slowly to the corner of the house to a spigot and turned on the sprinkler. Out came a gush of the water. She continued to laugh under her breath, thinking to herself that she turned off one gush a moment earlier only to turn on another. She was used to his antics and, for each of them, she adored him.

The next day was beautiful. The sun was so bright and alluring, it was as if it cast a challenging spell on those in the neighborhood; everyone had emerged to manicure their yard in some manner. On days like this, Ted usually found himself talking with one or two other male neighbors in the middle of the street. The topic of choice was always grass: cutting it, growing it or caring for it. How best to take care of a lawn in all seasons seemed to be a hot concern for this *ad hoc* group. Usually there would be one resident expert who enjoyed dispensing knowledge about all lawn care subjects. His lawn may or may not have been the best looking fescue on the block... But his advice was free. Ted, despite being amused by the whole parade of knowledge, always listened intently.

"This weed that you're talking about... is it kinda blue? Did it come up as your grass was growing, after you spread the fertilizer? If it is, you'd be wasting your money putting that bag of stuff on it—it won't kill the weed," Ted's neighbor bellowed.

Ted, eager to be involved, piped up, "With that in mind, grass seed comes with seeds of weed and no one seems to mind. Why is that? We all knowingly buy bags of grass seed that have five percent weed seed. But just like us all, nothing is perfect." The neighbors stared blankly, moving on to discuss the latest products at the local home and garden store.

Ted was fully aware that there was always some new product to spread on the lawn. From fertilizers, which now came in a variety of seasonal mixtures, like beer from micro breweries, to weed killers, crab grass preventers, lime, insecticides, and many other wonderful treatments that guaranteed to keep lawns near perfect, they instilled a sense of pride in the neighborhood's homeowners. Most on his street had invested in irrigation systems that watered like clockwork, even during a two-day monsoon.

But all of the talk never did much for Ted. It was something as individual as each blade of grass that held meaning to him. It was the simple practice of whiffing at will. The deeper the sniff, the greater the pleasure; but it's more than his olfactory that was benefiting. The smell, like many in our lives, triggered vivid memories for Ted: good memories, as intense as the scent itself.

———

Last summer, Ted's teenaged son had the pleasure of cutting their grass for the first time. Ted showed him the proper way to operate the mower, as his dad showed him, thinking of it as a rite of passage. "As the time comes, and a dad so deems that his son is ready to be entrusted with a loud, dirty machine wielding a large, sharp blade, it can only be thought of as a new adventure. Once realized, looking back is not an option," Ted had grandiosely thought.

The first time Zach squared up with the Toro, sparks flew. "Your lines are crooked, oh gosh they're crooked… stop the mower… he can't hear me," Ted screamed. "STOP THE MOWER!"

Once a few early hurdles were cleared, the ritual evolved to one that was safer, cleaner and altogether personal. Zach quickly got the hang of it, despite a few mishaps, such as running the mower over a couple of exposed oak tree roots, and forgetting to periodically empty the mower bag to prevent clumps. "Clumps of grass are never a good sight on a newly mowed lawn," Ted would echo.

After four or five times watching and closely observing his son through the wispy, camouflaged curtains of their dining room window, Ted realized that he, in fact, missed the grass, the sun and the roar of the motor. He hadn't realized how much he relished the moments of getting away from people with nothing but the mower, the yard and his thoughts—his own thoughts. He hoped that Zach could eventually understand and capture the spirit of the occasion and take pleasure in it, at least for a moment here and a minute there, like his old man.

—∞∞∞—

The next morning, Ted found himself looking out the kitchen window, gazing at birds of many delightful colors, feasting on a smorgasbord of seeds from Kirsten's "squirrel-proof" bird feeder. Despite the obstacles, some pesky squirrels disturbed the banquet, as a chipmunk scurried unnoticed, scooping up what morsels had fallen to the deck. Ted looked for a reason to join the critters in the backyard, so he grabbed his teenage daughter's magazine, as it was the only piece of reading material in reach, and hastily poured a cup of old coffee. He ambled out to the deck and deposited himself on his favorite Adirondack chair. The sun felt warm as it peaked through puffy gray clouds. The breeze seemed slow, but steady.

Ted hadn't been planted a moment when the frolic of his animal guests and the fresh solitude of the second was injected with the ruckus of his son and the mower. Trying not to be bothered, Ted sat back and sipped his stale coffee, thumbing through the magazine he didn't know had existed before that morning. "What is Steph reading these days?" It really didn't matter. All was fine.

A scent of grass clippings caught him by surprise, attached to a deliberate, steady breeze, delivered to him without fanfare. Placing the magazine in his lap, Ted laid his head against his high chair back and closed his eyes. Seeing red as the sun shone down on this face, he encountered more wafts, and with each, something deep in his mind was released. What came over him was another jab of memory that was all but forgotten, ferreting more and more out from behind other memories, as the scent of fresh cut grass enveloped the yard. Ted felt content with nothing but his thoughts.

Taking it all in, Ted was suddenly blitzed with memories from his youth. Thinking back, he remembered when he was his son's age, cutting grass for summer spending money. "Ah, spending money: that's all money was needed for in those days. Mortgages, insurance and car payments didn't exist. That was a great summer," Ted reminisced.

He remembered a hot, quiet summer day when he had ventured into the grass-cutting business. Ted was bored, his sixteen year-old friends away at camps or at the pool, and thought it was time to make some extra money. He had his eye on a new ten-speed. Grass cutting for older neighbors had seemed to be the thing to do.

"So you want to cut grass for a living," young Ted's dad had asked him. "Well I'll give you your first break. You can use *my* lawn mower at no charge if you keep it full of gas at *your* expense. Teddy, you have to invest first in yourself and your business. Remember another thing—listen to your customers, but stay true to yourself and your goals and enjoy what you do."

Young Ted was inpatient with his dad, as he had expected to merely take the old machine and start scouting for overgrown yards that needed him. But Ted's first lessons from his father, albeit obvious, were ones that he had always remembered.

Only a week or so after he had hung out his shingle, Teddy was pushing his dad's clanking Sears mower up his street, when a relic of a man waved his twisted fingers, motioning him to come closer. At the time, Teddy thought that the man must be a hundred—*he had to be*. A skinny man who must have been six feet tall in his youth was hunched over. For someone with poor posture, he moved gracefully, like the curved and twisting neck of a swan. His steel-blue eyes sparkled like glass as they were disproportionately magnified by his tiny wire frame specs hanging from his large question mark-shaped ears, and held steady by his bird-like nose. His freckled and discolored skin loosely hung on his face and neck and, with this, it was hard for Teddy to imagine this man as anything but who he was at that instant.

The old man wore wingtip shoes with a shine and old, baggy pants hiked up to his sunken chest almost to the penguin logo of the knit shirt. His pants were dark blue and his shirt was maroon—he appeared toasty warm on such a hot summer day. His straw fedora was the only item of clothing that gave Teddy any thought that the man was trying to stay cool.

Hesitant and scared to talk with what seemed to be the living dead, young Ted slowly approached the man, studying his cool eyes. His large eyes behind his thick lenses that were all he could see. Peering into his eyes, even as a teenager, Teddy knew there was more to this man than his ancient exterior.

"Young man. I'm looking for someone who knows how to work one of them things there to spruce up the yard," the man said in an unexpectedly high-pitched voice. He slowly turned to look at his yard. Still looking away, he continued, "I would like this person to mow my lawn once a week on Thursday mornings... at around ten. Yes, ten in the morning. I'm not looking for it to be messed with on Wednesday or some other day—you hear me?" he said in with a serious tone.

Thinking it was an odd request, Teddy remembered his dad telling him to listen to the customer. He informed the old man of his standard fare of six dollars, to which he hemmed and hawed but eventually agreed. Young Ted nodded, turned and walked away, puzzled. Teddy had no idea what those sweaty Thursday mornings in the summer of 1973 would eventually mean.

As requested, young Ted showed up every Thursday morning to take care of Mr. Sinclair's lawn, whether it needed it or not. Just like any other grass-cutting job, he found that he enjoyed being outside, letting his thoughts wander where they may. No one ever disturbed him.

Mr. Sinclair made a point of staying inside when Teddy worked in his yard. But for no apparent reason to Teddy, on the fourth Thursday, the old man sat in a rusted pale yellow lawn chair under a willow tree the whole hour, watching Teddy's every move. He was perched in his side yard with an unobstructed view of both the front and back yards. Teddy didn't like having a spectator, but overlooked the old man. On occasion, Mr. Sinclair would shout out something, and Teddy merely shook his head, not hearing what the old man was saying. For the first time, Teddy thought of Mr. Sinclair as a lonely man.

Upon completing his work that day, Teddy walked over to the old man. Mr. Sinclair's thin lips curled upward at their ends. "You join me for a Coca-Cola? Not waiting for the boy to answer, Mr. Sinclair slowly pulled himself up from his chair and continued, "give me a minute and meet me around back at the picnic table."

About ten minutes passed, and Teddy was beginning to worry about the old man but, at that instant, Teddy heard the squeak of the screen door opening. He noticed that Mr. Sinclair's hands were trembling holding two tall bottles of soda. Teddy met him half way and they both walked to the table and sat down. As he gave Teddy one of the cold wet bottles of Coke he said, "hold it out here," he grumbled, fumbling desperately to remove the metal cap with the bottle opener attached to the Swiss Army knife he pulled from his pocket. As Mr. Sinclair continued to struggle, Teddy grew more uncomfortable, not knowing what to do. He held the bottle as steady as he could and decided to stare intently at nothing else but the "C" on the bottle. "Keep looking at the C," he repeated to himself. All was quiet, except for the nicking noise of the metal opener clanking on the metal cap.

With no success, Mr. Sinclair finally stopped, bursting into laughter, immediately easing the tension they both felt. The old man's laughter was contagious, and instantly Teddy joined in. Still guffawing, he closed the knife and tossed it to Ted. They both smiled, easing themselves onto the bench.

They sipped from the bottles in silence. Birds chirped overhead and the noise of the occasional car disturbed the solitude of the moment. With no warning, Mr. Sinclair began to talk with Teddy in a way no adult had ever talked with him before. He was clearly older than Teddy's grandfather. Undoubtedly the oldest person he had ever known. He seemed genuinely interested in the boy—his likes, thoughts and ambitions. Likewise, young Ted found great interest in him. He told Ted of his days as a soldier in World War I, and how his family got through the Great Depression in a tenement building in the city.

"We didn't have two nickels to rub together," he noted with a solemn grimace. "Of course don't ask me why we would want to do that in the first place," he said with a smile. That unexpected comment sparked a chuckle from Teddy, as he now knew why the old man had paused before agreeing to pay his standard fare. "Six dollars… well it can buy about twelve Slurpees." Teddy had thought to himself "But I didn't think it was very much—a nickel was definitely nothing.

"We valued other things, just like what we're doing right here and now," Mr. Sinclair continued with an insightful tone. "We're sitting and jawboning and sharing the good and the bad. We had other values too. We valued an honest wage for an honest day of work. So do you," he said, smiling and pointing to Teddy. Mr. Sinclair took a long swig from the bottle. "We placed a value on dedication. So do you want to know why I asked you to come on Thursdays?" He paused and looked at his yard. A stream of perspiration slowly meandered down his cheek from under his hat. He then answered his own question. "Well, I wanted to see if you were dedicated and if I could count on you to come when I needed you the most.... And you did it," he said, shaking his head and wearing a proud grin. His face took on childlike warmth.

Mr. Sinclair continued, telling young Ted where he went to school and, later, that he graduated from professional school and became an architect.

"I don't care where you go to school as long as you go to school," he said, once again turning a serious tone. "You know what I mean? I'd take a young man in my firm with a B average from the local college faster than I would from my uppity alma mater. You know why? Well I'm gonna tell you why. Because I know that if you earn a B at the local college that you are experiencing life. A B at my fancy school means that you studied and studied and studied; I later learned that this was not the way."

Mr. Sinclair looked down and inspected his hands. Teddy noticed the purple blotched skin of his long arthritic fingers. His wedding band, still in place, glimmered in the sun's rays.

Switching topics, Mr. Sinclair spoke at length about his late wife: when he met her, where they lived and where they traveled. While he spoke his usual high-toned voice seemed more resonant and heavy.

"Bea was lovely and I miss her. I was a pain in the rump roast and she overlooked my pompous ways. We were good for each other—really we were," he expounded, a subtle tear welling in his eye. "She could have had a number of other beaus, but I think we were meant to have one another. She was practical, you see. I was all over the place, but we connected somehow." Mr. Sinclair took off his hat, revealing the few wet and matted strands on his mostly bald head. He held the crown of his fedora and fanned himself. "We traveled as my company grew, and my accounts were spread throughout the world. We did, however, make the most of the time we were together. Young man, that is another value," He stated profoundly.

Mr. Sinclair stood up and, as he would do many times, shifted his thoughts to another subject. "What's more, I graduated first in my class, and I headed up a powerful business, but that junk doesn't matter. Experiences are meaningless if one does not become something from those experiences. It's who a person becomes, not those things that happened to him, that made him who he was. Let me tell you, acquiring wealth did nothing to define my character." Teddy didn't mind Mr. Sinclair's tendency to orate, as he felt sure he had the right to do so.

Teddy didn't know what Mr. Sinclair was like in his early years, but when he knew him, he was a gentle soul—perhaps Mr. Sinclair's finest moments. It was just the two of them every Thursday, whether Mr. Sinclair's lawn needed mowing or not. Each time they enjoyed a soda, and each time they said goodbye, with more thoughts and questions for their next encounter. It had become the best part of the summer for Teddy. Mr. Sinclair looked forward to Thursday.

Ted thought as he sat in his Adirondack chair, running through his teenage conversations with the old man. "I must have guessed that one day, when I was older, I would remember my conversations with Mr. Sinclair and think about what he said." Extending his legs out and crossing them at his ankles, and locking his fingers together behind his head, Ted thought more. "I definitely didn't have patience or maturity then, but my intuition recognized that I should hang onto those thoughts. Ah, hearing the grind of the machine in the hands of my son, it makes me realize the meaning of those conversations."

One particular conversation surfaced in Ted's mind, vividly replaying itself in his mental theater. He remembered Mr. Sinclair telling him, with one of his signature grins, "I designed some whoppers and engineered some massive buildings. Most are still standing, and will for many years. I say—so what! Yes, it was a wonderful life, and the challenges were inspiring. But these colossal buildings are hollow monuments."

Young Ted hadn't known what he meant but forty-seven-year-old Ted probed his thought further.

"What was it that Mr. Sinclair said again that time? Oh yeah, something like, "what I realized, later in life, was that the permanence of my own self worth came from the all kinds of people I met who wanted to be in my life. Only later did I muster the courage to act on my feelings." Ted sat up and forward closing his eyes trying to drill deeper into his memory. "What did he say after that? What was it… oh yeah, "Something clicked in me and I realized that it's about flesh and bones, and not bricks and mortar. I made changes in my career and rewrote my personal definition of what I could do as builder. I learned life was more than constructing buildings using cold metal, concrete and glass, to make a lot of money."

Sitting back in the chair, Ted began mumbling to himself, "Come to think of it, I don't think Mr. Sinclair ever put any fertilizer or crabgrass preventer on his lawn... When Zach finishes this week's "one on one" with the lawn, maybe I'll tell him this story, or better yet, I'll urge him to make some summertime money and find a Mr. Sinclair."

Example moves the world more than doctrine.
– Henry Miller

The years teach much which the days never knew.
– Ralph Waldo Emerson

Years only teach us when we find value in the thread of moments that lead to today. Overnight success is seldom overnight. True discovery takes time; self-discovery may take a lifetime.

MEKO'S SALVAGE AND REPAIR

There is a crack in everything God has made.
> – Ralph Waldo Emerson

Truth is something you stumble into when you think you are going someplace else.
> – Jerry Garcia

God is in the details.
> – St. Augustine

The important thing is to do, and nothing else; be what it may.
> – Pablo Picasso

Do not wish to be anything but what you are, and try to be that perfectly,
> – St. Francis De Sales

Bending his long torso in half, with one hand pressed into the rocky asphalt and the other on the side of his car, Charles peered at the shadowy underbelly of his car. He wanted to find out, once and for all, where it could be coming from. He was embarrassed that every morning, when he drove to work he left behind a growing oval puddle of oil.

Unaware that he was being watched, a neighbor out jogging stopped his run to lend unsolicited advice.

"Take it to Meko's," Mick roared in a booming voice. His sudden appearance and pronouncement startled Charles. Jumping to his feet and wiping his hair out of his eyes, he said, "I was thinking about taking it to the dealership."

"Oh, I'd never take it to the dealership. When my Volvo has a problem and I can't fix it, I take it in to see Arnold. Charles, have you tried fixing it yourself?"

Surprised by the question, Charles confessed, "oh… no. I'm not really good that way. If I can't see the problem right away, then I'm trouble."

"I understand. I grew up with my head under the hood or under the chassis. I cut my teeth on some really old cars, so if I couldn't find the problem, I'd fish around and find the answer," Mick offered.

Charles told Mick of his experience, thinking that he might offer to help him. "Well, about a year ago, I took it to the dealership and the mechanic told me to keep adding oil every other week, as needed. And he went on to say he could fix it, but it'd cost at least twelve hundred dollars and he could NOT guarantee that what he would do to it would take care of the problem."

"Pretty steep for an oil leak. See, I wouldn't have taken it to the dealership. That's why I'm telling you about Arnold."

Rolling with frustration from one thought to the next, Charles continued, "on top of that, the Volvo guy told me that to replace my lost wheel cover would be sixty-five dollars. That was just like adding salt to my wound. I mean that's just a piece of plastic."

"Wow, I see maybe it's a good idea to take it to someone you can trust," Mick said as he started running in place.

"You're right. I'm telling you, talk to Arnold. I don't know what he'd charge you, but it won't be anywhere near twelve hundred—and he'll guarantee his work."

Charles finally heard Mick's message. He settled himself down and shook his head at his suggestion. Mick, after all knew about cars, and Charles presumed he trusted Arnold.

Charles was in his mid thirties, and was a good six and half feet tall, and each inch was ganglier than the last. His exceptionally straight auburn bangs frequently flopped in his eyes, like a sheepdog's. Charles double-checked everything, because most of what he did was either black or white. This trait came in handy, as he worked with lots of numbers, especially during tax time. He tended to apply the same approach when working with people. Sometimes his self-perceived strength would be an obstacle.

In the past year Charles and his wife, Emma, moved into the neighborhood, and were expecting their first baby, so a quart of oil every so often, and three hub caps, seemed just fine. Up until the time Mick stopped by, Charles felt he could trust the advice given him from the clean-cut, articulate and sharp mechanic at the dealership.

After talking to Mick moments earlier, Charles took advantage of the unusually cool and bright day, to sit on his front steps thinking about what Mick told him. He weighed his advice against the words of the mechanic at the dealership. Blowing his breath into his clasped hands to warm them, he stared at his car in front of him and thought of the pool of oil it now covered. Thinking he should at the very least talk to someone at Meko's, Charles went to the kitchen, pulled out the drawer where they kept the phone directory and flipped open the yellow pages.

He muttered to himself, "Meko, Meko—is that with an e-c or e-k?" He couldn't readily find a listing for Meko's. He then checked the white pages and there he found a one-line listing—Meko's—and the phone number; nothing more. He dialed the number and it rang six or seven times. As he was about to hang up, he heard a raspy and guttural female voice on the other end. It was the kind of sound that was lubricated with a fair share of coffee and cigarettes over the years.

"Meko's, this is Belinda, can you hold please?" Not waiting for an answer, the next thing Charles knew he was on hold. Not expecting to be put on hold, Charles was bothered and considered hanging up, but decided to wait it out. What in the world does she look like? Not ten seconds later, she returned.

Charles asked for an appointment and, with a snicker, she told him, "Sweetheart, just bring it on by and we'll let you know what we can do."

This comment was unsettling for Charles. I make appointments for everything these days— doctor, haircuts, CPA, dog grooming, plumber— what does she mean? He seemed to resolve himself regarding their manners and, as she continued, Charles conceded to give Meko's a try.

"Just bring it in on Monday, and Arnold will work you in," She gave him directions, and he meticulously wrote down every turn and mile estimate. Later that afternoon, he went online to search for directions, but came up with two scenarios other than what Belinda told him.

On Monday, Charles opted to use her directions and followed her every turn. Not too far from where he lived, but in an area that was unfamiliar to him, he approached a road under construction and a flagman signaled him to take a detour. What the heck... I may not be able to find my way if this flagman sends me down that street. But with no choice, other than turning and going back the way he came from, he proceeded down a gravel street. He stopped at a railroad track and slowly crossed the rails. As a result of his anxiety, his fear seemed to become his reality—he was lost, or so he thought.

He pulled over to the side of the overly crowned road with plumes of black smoke pouring from under the hood. Soon to follow the haze, the stink of oil on hot greasy metal filled the air. Good grief. Rubbing his eyes with one hand, and pulling out his cell phone with the other, Charles glanced out his window to find what looked like a large dilapidated airplane hanger. Beguiled by the sight, he got out of his car and looked around. To his astonishment, he was close to the highway he drove daily to and from downtown. He could also see, in the distance, the roofs of the new upscale shopping mall in the other direction. To him, he was someplace different, but so very near to the world in which he was comfortable. Never before did he venture from the established roads that others paved so neatly. Looking at his immediate surroundings, he observed that, unlike the mall and the neighborhood he was accustomed to, these buildings around him were hideous and ancient. This place should be condemned. The rusted out trucks and trailers from a time long ago littered the area as if in a forgotten war zone, with each a story could be told. Stalks of weed sprouted from the ashen color and cracked asphalt that speckled the area. It dawned on him that he wasn't lost. He was only seventy-five paces or so from Meko's. The dead giveaway for him was the huge red letters, although now faded pink, "Meko's Salvage and Repair" painted across one wall.

He surprised himself, as he felt a tinge of reverence walking through what he thought of as the final resting place of at least one-hundred-plus

Volvos of every vintage. It was eerie, as he heard only the song of field birds and the breeze whishing through the irregular and misshapen brush that grew there. But the hum of the traffic of the distant highway reminded him of where he came from. Is this place even open?

After wending through Volvo carcasses, he approached a screen door like one he would find on someone's back porch. This one, though, dangled on only two of its three hinges and behind it was gray steel door framed with rivets. Gently pulling the doors open, he crossed the threshold and, to his immediate right, he saw an old service counter made of pressed wood paneling that was dutifully damaged by forty years of insults. Calendars adorned with photos of monster automobiles and trucks with huge tires draped the walls. Worn Pennzoil posters, barely hanging on by yellowed tape, covered other cinder block walls. A fifty-some-year-old lady chatted on the phone, while two middle-aged mechanics sat on unsteady stools talking to each other. One drank coffee, and the other a Big Gulp. All were puffing on cigarettes. Charles, in his gray flannel suit and yellow club necktie hanging well above his belt buckle, stood with patience at the counter. One of the mechanics, a wiry red- and gray-haired man, teetering on one of the stools, waved to Charles. Using his own form of sign language, as his soft drink sloshed from out of his super-sized cup. Charles interpreted his hand movements as "hello sir; she'll get to you just as soon as she's off the phone. Thanks for your patience". Well-mannered as always, Charles nodded with a forced smile. He couldn't help to begin to think if he was now wasting his time—after all weren't, those Volvos dead out there? What was Mick thinking of when he sent me here?

Belinda, behind the counter, said her good-byes, hung up the phone and walked toward Charles. She was the one and the same who Charles spoke with a few days earlier by phone. Her voice was very recognizable. Friendly and warm, she asked Charles to walk across the hall to the Repair Department. She made it clear to him that he was currently in the Salvage Department.

"Arnold will be right with you," she said as he was walking away. Charles walked down the hall to the Repair Department.

Poking his head around the door jam, he saw that no one was in the small room. On dusty shelves, he saw old car parts and pieces, among other remnants. To one side, he saw archaic company trophies awarded for bowling and auto competitions. Some had images of cars emblazoned on them. A stack of new tires was in one corner, and wrenches and other tools, thrown in a heap, in another. Everything seemed to be covered with grime, and he was beginning to feel that way too.

Ushered back in time, beginning subtly with Mick's recommendation two days earlier, Charles's feelings of misgiving were anything but dissuaded, but he was pulled in like a magnet. He decided to sit down and make himself comfortable on a bench seat of a 1970 240 sedan. Except for the laughter floating in from the Salvage Department, and the muffled and static sound of a radio drifting in from the garage, all was quiet. It was far too quiet for a place that was designed to fix broken cars. Anxious over his thoughts, Charles let out a sigh and picked up a four-year-old copy of Field and Stream magazine he found on the floor where he was sitting.

Just at that moment, a short, scrawny man with a ponytail walked into the room. He was out of breath, and plopped down next to Charles. He yanked off his washed-out and crumpled cap and scratched his wrinkled forehead with his discolored pinky nail. He grumbled, "I'm too old for this— way too old." Worn around the edges, but he was younger than his looks conveyed.

Charles, with trepidation and trying to appear invisible, peered over and saw that the man sitting next to him had the name 'Arnold' printed in all caps in the oval above his pocket. Charles, without drawing attention, leaned forward and slowly started to stand up hoping to go unnoticed. But before he could, Arnold jumped to his feet and introduced himself. He knew Charles was waiting for him.

"I'm gonna take a look at your car right now. You'll need to leave it with me for a day. Warren, who runs one of our tow trucks, will see to it you get to work. You do work, don't you?" Arnold asked, lightheartedly.

Like a cornered rabbit, Charles nodded. "Ah… yeah, that'd be great."

Arnold held his palm up to Charles, signaling for him to stay where he was, and he walked over to the door opening to the garage and, leaning on one foot, he poked his head out the door leading to the bays, and called for

Warren. "Hey Warren, I need you to run Charles downtown while we take a look at his vehicle."

Charles detected no audible answer.

Arnold said something under his breath that Charles could not hear. Arnold added to his request, "Hey buddy, you owe me."

Charles, sensing that he was imposing on this man, whom he had yet to meet, spoke up with apprehension, "Arnold, if Warren isn't suppose to give rides, I understand—please."

Arnold laughed, "no, no—it's Warren's job. He's just needs a pot of coffee and a kick in the butt to get going. You understand."

Warren was a white-haired elderly gentleman who wore a black Greek fisherman's hat and a Members Only jacket. His bulbous nose was difficult to discount when talking with him. Walking with a slight limp, he traveled past the two, headed for the front door. His gait was steady and swift. He nodded to Charles and kept walking to the door.

"Charles, you better catch up with him or he'll leave you behind." Arnold said in all seriousness. Once that dawned on Charles, he ran to catch up.

He followed Warren across the lot to a large baby-blue tow truck that matched Warren's jacket. It was clearly marked, MEKO'S. As Charles opened his door, a paper cup with some foul liquid tumbled to the pavement.

"Sorry about that. Hope it didn't get on ya," Warren said with some concern in his low voice. He then mumbled, "I'll have to find me another spit cup somewheres."

Charles hoisted himself high into the cab and, as he was positioning himself in his seat, he became aware of the stuffing coiling from the creases of the cold vinyl seats. Not cleaned for some time, the ash tray was brimming with butts and paper napkins, and fast food bags were balled up on the floor. With a forceful yank, they pulled the doors shut, one after the other, and a hollow echo of metal on metal bounced around in the over-sized cab. This was a mammoth towing machine that could handle transporting large trucks.

With exception of the typical highway noises, the clatter of the bouncing tow trucks, and with the occasional radio dispatcher chatter, the twenty-minute drive was uneventful. Very few words were spoken, although Charles tried to make small talk. But Warren merely nodded or grunted. As they pulled up to the building where Charles worked, Warren suddenly found his voice.

"You're business is appreciated, and Arnold and the rest of us will take mighty good care of you. You have a great day, sir, and it was my pleasure toting you to work." Warren completed his soliloquy with a genuine smile that showed a great deal of his dentures. Charles said "thank you", nodded his head and smiled back.

By the time Charles stepped in his office, he noticed the voice mail message light was blinking. It was Arnold. He discovered the problem. He needed Charles to call him and he did so at once.

"I'm sorry to tell you, but I'm going to have to pull your engine apart to fix the leak. It's the rear main and it is a big, I mean big, job," Arnold said with a steady tone.

Charles still unsure of his decision answered with hesitation. "Well, I thought it would be a pretty big job. If it's too big for you to handle, that would be fine."

With a cigarette-stained laugh, Arnold said, "I did say it was a big job, but there's nothing I can't handle. I've been fixing these here cars since I was a teenager... if you want to come get it, though, that'd be fine with me. I've got my hands full."

"No, no, I just wasn't sure if you wanted to take care of it or not... what would a job like this run me?"

"Oh, I'll do my best to keep it under four hundred dollars, and I guarantee my work. If you have problems when you drive it off my lot, just bring it back and I'll take care of it at no extra cost," Arnold boasted.

Charles was dumbfounded. He told Arnold that he agreed to his terms, and Arnold told him he could pick it up that evening. Charles thought about this episode all day and, many times, thought perhaps Arnold was scamming him. The place was odd and very unprofessional, he thought. It looked like something out of the fifties. The people seemed comical. They seemed like they could be in a sitcom, he thought again. But what is it that I am judging them on anyway? Preoccupied the whole day, and thinking about his decision, he still wasn't sure if he trusted Meko's but he was intrigued by Arnold and his shop. There was something about Arnold that Charles could not pinpoint. By the end of the day, something inside Charles told him that he made a good decision by leaving his car with Arnold.

Charles found a ride from a co-worker that afternoon, and returned to Meko's at about five-thirty to pick up his car.

"Hey Charles," Belinda shouted when he entered the building as if she had known him for years. "Sorry, hon, but you're going to have to wait a spell. Take a load off and have a seat in the Repair Department." He did so, and sat where he was that morning. After a few minutes, he got up and took another look around the shop. This time, he looked more closely at everything in the room. He saw that Arnold's name was on most of the plaques and trophies. He walked up to the counter, placed his hands on its surface, and leaned forward to look at a bulletin board besieged with pictures of his family. Also tacked to the sides were a number of IOUs. Without looking, Charles moved his hand and knocked over a large plastic cylinder full of change and some bills. He noticed the container had writing on it. Fight Leukemia. This second look gave Charles some reassurance. As Charles resumed his seat, the wiry red- and gray-headed mechanic Charles spoke to earlier in the day tapped him on his shoulder.

"I've been helping Arnold on your vehicle, and we're in the final stages of the job. Hang on, sir, and we'll be finished soon. Looking out a small window, Charles realized the day was wearing thin, and the sky was already dark. He sat down.

After about twenty-five minutes of waiting, Charles had just read three articles in Field and Stream, when Arnold whisked in the room. Smudges outlined his face, and he used a greasy rag to wipe his hands, but to no avail.

"Whew, that was a mean one, but it's done—we fixed it. But if you do have problems, bring it on back and I'll work on it until I get it right. I didn't get all this by doing an average job," Arnold said while opening his arms and motioning around the shop.

"So what do I owe you?"

"I told you this morning—three hundred and ninety dollars." Arnold replied.

"You mean to tell me that you spent all day on my car and it was a bigger job than what you thought and you're still going with that price?"

"That's my story and I'm sticking to it—of course I am. You pay Belinda, up front at the counter, and I'll pull your car around to the front," Arnold said. Charles paid Belinda. "Hon, hope to see you again real soon... well, I don't mean I hope you have car problems, but it's a nice thing to say."

As Charles paid her he glanced out the window and saw the headlights of Warren's tow truck towing a car onto the property. Charles said goodbye to Belinda and walked outside and, as he did, Warren passed him giving him a wink and a wave. Arnold drove up, opening the door while still rolling. Like a valet, he closed the door behind Charles and off he went with a wave.

No black smoke, that's good, Charles thought. About ten minutes into the drive home he heard a rattle. His fuse was short and he felt his heart race. He was angry and was sure that his oil leak, fixed or not, cascaded to a new problem. "Thanks, Arnold," Charles muttered under his breath. Still fuming when he pulled up in front of his house, he threw open the car door and went around to the rear of his car to open the trunk, where he kept a flashlight. He wanted to look under the carriage to see if he could determine what was making the new noise. It seemed like it was coming from the back of the car. As he flipped open the trunk lid the light inside flickered on and with the dim light what he saw amazed him. There, causing the rattle, was a fourth wheel cover with a note.

"Thanks for the business. Please tell someone you trust to give me a call. The wheel cover's just a token of our appreciation."

As naturally as the oak bears an acorn and the vine a
gourd, a man bears a poem, either spoken or done.
— Henry David Thoreau

Make the most of yourself, for that is all there is to you.
— Ralph Waldo Emerson

If you would be a real seeker after the truth, it is necessary that at least once in your life you doubt, as far as possible, all things.

— René Descartes

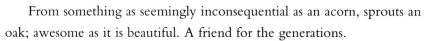

From something as seemingly inconsequential as an acorn, sprouts an oak; awesome as it is beautiful. A friend for the generations.

From humanity, like an acorn, comes a poem, but only with care. To care for is to care about. Truth and beauty are replaced by suspicion and gloom. But it doesn't have to be so.

An acorn looks little like its essence found inside, as well as by what eventually comes from it.

THE BUGGY MAN

*Truth has no special time of its own. Its hour is now—
always.*

– Albert Schweitzer

*A man should look for what is, and not what he thinks
should be.*

– Albert Einstein

"I was born just over that hill there, in that house. I can't be sure
though, I was too young to remember. But my family told me so," said an
old Amish man, pointing straight over Jake's right shoulder. Jake turned his
head, and all he could discern was the patina of a painted tin roof. For that
fleeting moment, Jake played with the thought of what it must be like to
grow to adulthood traveling only three to five miles from where you were
born, and relishing it enough to sense pride in revealing it to a stranger.
Roused by the moans of his impatient son, Jake shook his head affirmatively
at the old man, and turned and grimaced at his young teenager.

Jake and Heather were on vacation with their four children. They had a
notion that spring to take an old-time summer vacation. They packed the
mini van, as they remembered their parents before them packed the station
wagon, decided on several stops between points somewhere else and home
again, to stop and take in the sights.

"No major interstates," Jake proclaimed to Heather. "I want to take the
scenic route. Those old roads will get us to where we need to go. Don't you
think?"

Heather, who planned most of their trips, was excited about the proposition, and sent for a number of maps of the mid-Atlantic. "Oh, I agree with you, Jake. This will be fun. There are many roads that will get us where we want to go."

When Jake and Heather announced their vacation plans to the children, their two teenagers thought they were being ambushed.

"What!" Brian, their oldest child protested. "I thought we were going someplace fun."

"No beach? This is going to be a real drag. How'm I supposed to get a tan?" Colette, their middle school daughter added.

"We're going to have loads of fun. Just wait and see. . We've got Washington's home, we have a hike planned in Delaware…c'mon, and we have some great times ahead of us. We might even learn something," Jake said with conviction.

"This is gonna be like a major field trip," Brian said with disgust.

Their first stop on their car trip was Lancaster, Pennsylvania, where Jake decided they would take a buggy ride. They parked and slowly emerged from the mini van.

Jake motioned to his son to pick up his pace and join the rest of his family, all sitting together on a redwood picnic table bench. There they sat under a primeval knotted and twisted oak tree, as they waited for the next buggy to take them through the Pennsylvania countryside. Jake and Heather's oldest daughter joined their son, emitting her own sounds of exasperation accentuated by her crossed arms, with her head turned to one side, leaning her weight on one foot. Their two youngest daughters ran laps around them, laughing hysterically. They knew how to make the most of the moment.

Grinning widely, the old man watched the little ones. He caught Jake's attention and introduced himself as Aaron. Jake, of course, reciprocated, and shook Aaron's large and callused hand. As Aaron spoke to Jake, sweat on the old man's forehead glistened in the sun's hot rays. Each drop ran down his face and was trapped by his long gray and silver beard. Every now and again, he wiped his forehead and the back of his neck with a plain white handkerchief he would tug from the back pocket of his dungarees. For early in the morning, the sun was intense, as they waited with varying levels of patience for their excursion. The haze hung heavy in the air and the humidity was like an unwanted guest. But farmland in the distant hills appeared fresh and green.

Their time came, and the family of six was ready for the next ride. As another buggy approached the hitching post, Jake, keeping himself from staring, caught a glimpse of Aaron as he conversed with the other soon-to-be passengers, and witnessed a tenderness showing in his face. The deep lines in his forehead nearly met those rising from his cheeks, especially when he smiled, which often happened. His eyes were clear and childlike and, when talking with him earlier, Jake saw nothing but his eyes. Now, from a distance, Jake assembled a more inclusive picture of Aaron.

As they waited to board the buggy, other tourists who completed their ride, hopped out of the midnight black buggy and said farewell and thank you to the driver.

Aaron walked to the front of the buggy and approached the driver. The two men began to speak in a unique language called Pennsylvania Dutch. Jake couldn't help to think they were commenting on all the "English", as they called all those who were not Amish. As their ways seemed foreign to the sightseers, Jake was doubly certain the sightseers' actions were strange to the Amish.

While standing in line, waiting for the buggy to approach, Jake recalled other English of all ethnicities and races peering at the Amish people as if they were novelties, and perhaps they were in one sense, but it showed him something about the English. In this case, the complexities of the English were upended by simple and plain of the Amish.

It was time for Jake's group to begin boarding the buggy. This buggy was more like a wagon, but very much in the same style as what most English think of as a traditional Amish buggy, with a hard, flat roof with windows. The Amish constructed these buggies using clean, straight lines long before "clean, straight lines" were fashionable. Neither fashion nor style had to do with what they built. Simple and plain steer everything—simple and plain.

A great number of people from an extended family climbed on board, and Jake and his five followed. The passengers boarded as if they were jumping on a subway in midtown Manhattan. Although four of Jake and Heather's family were able to flow with the onslaught, Jake realized that there was no more room for him and their littlest girl. Jake looked at his Heather, and he confidently shook his head and waved, while mouthing that the two of them would wait for the next buggy. Seeing that Jake was separated from his family, Aaron walked over to where Jake was standing, and suggested that Jake climb up front with the driver, and his daughter could join him. She sat on a tiny three-legged wooden stool between Jake's legs. When the little girl heard this solution, she clasped her hands together, and her face lit up like it was Christmas day.

"Nothing should separate a family," Aaron said.

The gentle driver introduced himself as Isaac, while negotiating the two gleaming brown steeds away from the battered iron hitching post. While talking to both his passengers and the horses, he maneuvered the buggy around the grassy field and, finally, onto the main road. At once, like day turning to night, the passengers heard the cadence of the hooves authoritatively strike the asphalt. It was a rhythm that is seldom heard but lightens the spirit.

Once situated, Isaac asked everyone to introduce themselves, as the eighteen wheelers hauled down the road next to them, with no real concern for anything, except for their cargo and a deadline. Jake now knew what it was like to feel completely defenseless, as nothing but a thin plank of wood was the only barrier between him and his family and some very large anti-Amish vehicles. Jake looked at Isaac for comfort as he paid strict attention to the competing traffic. But he did announce to the group that he may not be able to talk too much until he could pull onto an Amish side road.

A mile or so down the road, it was time to leave the hustle of the highway and pull onto Amish thoroughfares. When the time came, it was as if the buggy magically entered a Grandma Moses painting—it was hard to believe they were just on the edge of the hurry-up and multitasking of the modern world. The narrow crowned street was bordered with thick, tall stalks of corn, unpretentious homes and functional farm buildings. Nary an eighteen-wheeler could be found.

Isaac, a tall older man with a closely cropped beard, with no mustache, was very personable. He wore the customary straw hat all men wear in the fields in the summer months. His royal blue shirt was crisp, and his black pants were held up by suspenders. He looked warm, but did not complain. He was old-order Amish, so his dress reflected his beliefs. His beliefs were reflected in his way. His way was simple.

"Feel free to take photographs at the beauty of the land, but not of the Amish people, as we believe photos are graven images and are sinful," said. He emphasized the beauty of the land—as is, simple, plain and untouched, except to be worked and tilled to bring sustenance for people.

"You can take from her, but you need to give back to her more than what you take," Isaac told his guests. Jake immediately thought of the Native Americans and the American family farmer who also felt deeply about our earth. That way, he thought seemed to be disappearing.

The horse's pace lightened to a walk, and Isaac asked for questions. An older lady in large sunglasses, with a huge pocketbook resting neatly on her lap asked with utter politeness, "What else do Amish people believe?"

"Well, the origin of the Amish people comes from Simon Menno a Catholic monk,, who left that religion several hundred years ago because he believed man should take the teachings of the Bible in a literal sense. At the time another man, Jacob Amman, felt man should not only take the Bible literally, but should view it with strict adherence. Thus, those who followed Menno became Mennonites and those who followed Amman became Amish."

"If I may ask another question, I would like to know more specifically some of your beliefs," the older lady asked.

"We believe in Jesus Christ, that he rose from the dead, to keep Sunday holy, and in adult baptism. For those of you who are Christian, you may think, and you would be correct, that we have many things in common. But it is the manner in which we live our life, to help us to stay faithful to God, perhaps is the real difference between us and other Christian religions."

As they strolled through the country roads, the green corn husks were high, and danced in unison in the warm breezes. The rolling landscape flowed and merged gracefully into the horizon. A few black birds flew over-head, with only the clomping of the hooves, and the creaking of the wooden wagon wheels leading to a meditative state. It was short-lived but therapeutic. Jake could only imagine what went through the heads of the others and, for that matter, what Isaac was thinking.

Approaching a home tucked to one side of the road, Isaac led the buggy down a narrow path where they came to a stop. A barefooted, and plainly dressed woman, and several girls, introduced themselves. Without a Madison Avenue pitch, they offered the sale of home-made cookies, pretzels, dolls and dish towels. All items were of remarkable quality and fancied a style all their own. In a way, the brand was recognizable and plainly "Amish" to the naked eye. A young girl gave Aaron a sandwich wrapped in a napkin. They spoke Pennsylvania Dutch briefly.

As they waited for a few minutes longer at the home for fresh cookies that Heather was buying, Jake admired the comfortable, but austere, home. Each home, one after the other that they saw, lacked electricity and many of the modern conveniences that go hand in hand with electrical power. No television, CD players, hair dryers, washing machines, or dishwashers would be found in these homes. Jake thought of those times when the electricity had abruptly vanished in their home and how they were inconvenienced. Our dependence, he thought, on things like electricity to perpetuate our complex lifestyle is somewhat regressive—not progressive.

Jake compared his life to what he imagined took place in the homes merely fifty feet from where the buggy was at rest. He thought of those moms passing down the cookie recipe and baking those cookies with their daughters. Jake imagined what it was like to learn the oral recipe of pretzels told from one generation to the next, and then to make those pretzels with mom and sisters. Jake thought of the young girls learning to sew and design dolls and mastering the art of making towels as well as their clothes. We're definitely trying to get rid of the human element in society. What—we run down to the store and spend a lot of money on cheaply made stuff. Isn't being human about the people? Jake's thoughts were bouncing in his head.

Once again they were on their way, and Isaac asked them, "What kind of work do you good folk do?"

Someone said they worked for a university. Another lawyer and yet another person said they were retired from government jobs. Ray, a younger man with a trendy haircut, wearing a muted expensive shirt and sleek slip-on leather shoes, announced that he worked for Google. Isaac asked in all sincerity, "What's a Google?"

"Google—it's the online browser, you know...?"

"No, I'm sorry Ray, I do not. Tell me, what is it that you do?"

"Well, I'm in PR and marketing."

"Uh huh. PR you said? And marketing? And computers."

A bit arrogant, Ray began to describe computers, but he was interrupted.

"Okay I know what a computer is, thanks Ray." Everyone but Ray chuckled, as they could hear playfulness in Isaac's voice. They also heard in his voice that he didn't much care to learn about Google, as he saw little relevance in Google to his life.

They rode past a two-story, one hundred-year-old barn. Although it was old, it looked well taken care of, as it was freshly painted red. Inside it were whirling fans hanging from the rafters, keeping all inside as cool as could be on an Amish farm.

Ray piped up, "well, Isaac, how do you generate those fans without electricity?" Ray presumably thought they must have been powered by electrical current. Isaac told the passengers that much is done in the home and on the farm using pneumatics not electricity.

"Ah...pneumatics? Now explain why the Amish don't use electricity. Is it considered evil," Ray asked sarcastically. Ray was in his late twenties and accompanying his parents who remained stone quiet during the entire tour.

"Don't worry about it, Ray. That's a question that comes up every buggy ride. Thanks for being the one asking this time." Again the English laughed at one of their own. Isaac continued, "The Amish don't use electricity because it is produced on Sundays, and we honor and revere Sunday, not because electricity is inherently bad. Electricity isn't evil, and we do not judge others who use it. We don't think that people who produce it on Sundays are evil either. We just prefer not to use it for that reason. It's really that simple.

They rode on in comfortable silence. Jake looked down at his little daughter, and her little face looked pure, as her eyes took in all that was before her. All was new to her, and to those who wanted to see. She heard none of the sarcasm, but listened to the messages brought to her without judgment.

Turning onto an even smaller road, Isaac began to speak, "Perhaps you should be aware of additional reasons that set us apart from others. Well, we live and let live—we do not judge. We do not try to convert you, nor do we believe in violence. We believe in turning the other cheek. I believe that might set us apart from other Christians and other religions of the world. As I mentioned a while back, we believe in using just enough of the earth's resources to live, and we believe in giving back to it. Farming is living."

Between questions, Jake talked with Isaac. He asked him about his work, and Jake asked about his. He told Jake that he was a school teacher, and that there were at least fifty one-room school houses in the area, spaced about every two to three miles. Parents pay two hundred dollars per year, and all the children walk to school.

"Even if you hadn't told us, I would have guessed you were a teacher. You communicate with such spirit. Every word means something," Jake told Isaac in a low quiet voice.

Isaac was about to respond to Jake, but their quiet conversation was interrupted. "Isaac, I have a question," blurted Ray from the back of the carriage.

"Good Ray, I've been waiting. What is it?"

"I saw one of those red and yellow cozy coops in the yard we just passed and, since that is made of plastic—you need electricity to make plastic—how do you explain that?"

"First Ray, what is a cozy coop?"

"It's a toy car that a kid sits in and powers it by moving their feet."

"Oh, I see. Do you have children, Ray?" Isaac said with a gentle utterance.

"No, I'm not married."

"Well, Ray there's hope for you yet. You may want to join the Amish and learn more about us." Laughter resounded from all in the buggy. Even Ray reluctantly smiled, as he realized he was not taken seriously by anyone.

As before, Isaac spoke calmly, "Ray, the Amish do not intentionally purchase items that they think are made on Sunday. We know others work on

Sunday. We do not judge them. We do our best to do what we think is right. That's my answer." His response was underscored by the placid rustle of the burgeoning stalks of corn on either side of the buggy that temporarily swept the visitors into an uncommon way of thinking. It was enchanting.

Isaac rubbed his eyes with his powerful fingers and spoke again, "Oh yes, one more thing. We are not perfect. I don't find that to be a bad thing, either, as I have found nothing man has made to be perfect. Tell me Ray, is the internet perfect?" This time the tourists howled with laughter in agreement with Isaac's sentiment.

After the laughter died down, Jake asked a question, "What do you do for fun? Say when the work is done, what do you look forward to doing?"

Turning to Jake with an oversized and well-intentioned smile, Isaac answered, "the work is never done. Oh, we have some time to laugh and play, especially when the family comes together for a picnic, but I make time to hug and kiss my little ones before they sleep. I spend time with my wife sitting on our porch and we talk. I don't separate any of that out—I enjoy it all. Better yet, I feel joy every day. Don't you?"

Jake thought about the question. "I try. I try to do the best I can." Jake looked back to the other four of his family members. Heather smiled and, as if embarrassed, Brian and Colette kept their heads down.

Jake turned to look at the passengers. "That's all we can do. We must try and try again. The Amish don't have a secret. Remove some clutter and keep trying. Funny thing, but eventually we all know what's important, no matter where we come from."

Their trip was over before any of the party wanted it to be—except perhaps Ray. Jake remembered that the simple trip was full of riches, mostly due to what he experienced through Isaac's eyes.

Upon completion of the journey, while the passengers disembarked, Isaac pulled Jake aside. "Jake I can tell you are a happy man. What a fine family you and your wife have. Try and try and try and the best will come."

"Thanks, sir."

Later that day, as Jake and Heather and their four children were driving to their next vacation destination, Jake looked through the rearview mirror and saw that Brian and Colette were being entertained with wires coming

Edward G. Kardos   93

out of their ears, and the little girls were watching a movie on a DVD player. He thought as he drove: We are convinced that we can't live without our things. But technology doesn't help us feel. A buggy and a teacher can do that. Multi-tasking accomplishes little—nothing like what comes from the Amish farmer or the Amish wife. Isaac told me that the work is never done. There's nothing like speaking what is true.

Jake took the next exit off the interstate.

"Do we need gas?" Heather asked.

"No, we don't need gas."

"Then what's wrong? Why are you stopping?" Heather was perplexed, as the children were mesmerized by their technology.

"I'm looking for the proper place to put something." Punctuating that statement with a sudden stop in front of a fast food restaurant, Jake threw open his car door and this children's. He pulled the DVD from their little hands and proceeding to rid his car of technological distractions and attachments, tossed them in the stinking, fly-infested barrel.

"Oh, and honey," Heather said with smile," don't forget about your Blackberry."

Jake, looking her in the eyes, was reminded why he married her. "Boy, you're tough… but right." Knowing there was no going back, Jake dislodged his ball and chain and heaved it with delight into the woods adjacent to where they stood, he himself free.

He painted what was there. The marmalade jar stayed where the last person had left it at breakfast. Nothing strained or contrived. Ordinary scenes, yes, but the ordinary painted with loving attention packed an extraordinary wallop.

–Author Sue Bender describing
the artwork of Fairfield Porter
in her book *Plain and Simple*

All the way to Heaven is Heaven

– St. Catherine of Siena

*I want to go soon and live away by the pond, where I
shall hear only the wind whispering among the reeds. It
will be a success if I shall have left myself behind*
– Henry David Thoreau

Transported to a place in which the words, faith, hope and love are cool, doesn't seem so bad. Can we leave our baggage, including headphones and cell phones behind, and still be in touch? Could heaven be before us and we can't see it? Ordinary scenes are only our beginning.

TOUCH NOT TECH

Life's most persistent and urgent question is, what are you doing for others.

— Aristotle

The best way to find yourself is to lose yourself in the service of others.

— Mahatma Gandhi

Upon the conclusion of a three-month project, completed at the office the day before, Nick found himself in the odd position of being at home on a Thursday morning. Feeling good that the new computer system was up and tested multiple times, running smoothly, and installed a week earlier than scheduled, he was ready for a break. Carrie was still asleep when Nick threw on his tattered Abercrombie hiking shorts, loafers and faded and shapeless navy Polo shirt. In the same vein as inhaling his next breath, he attached his Blackberry on this belt and grabbed his iPod. He tiptoed to the bathroom. Leaning forward to study his face in the mirror, he ran his fingers through his wavy dark brown hair, brushed his teeth with his Sonicare and with a jolt of inspiration, he decided to surprise Carrie that morning. Careful not to wake her, he hopped in his Lexus he bought with his last bonus, popped in a Bare Naked Ladies CD, and drove a half mile to the nearest Starbuck's—*I just love technology; it rocks!* Thinking of his recent accomplishment at work as he drove, he felt confident that most everything that could be thrown his way, he could handle.

Logical thinker, Nick was the project manager for his firm's most demanding clients. Younger than most he worked with, he was considered the fair-haired boy of the company, as he was able to make software and hardware do almost everything imaginable. Only with the firm less than two years, he was up for promotion.

Carrie was a tall slender woman with chestnut hair when she and Nick met. She was in her last year of physical therapy school at the time. Introduced by mutual friends, they were inseparable from the moment they met.

She grew up in a military family, and never spent much time in any one place. Her warm hazel eyes and genuine disposition made her friends and co-workers on Main 1-East at the hospital feel welcomed and engaged. Carrie was enthralled with her work. As her patients grew from despondency to optimism, she felt she grew too, and her altruistic nature was present in all she did. Without much thought, she relied on her innate abilities to accomplish whatever she put her mind to. Nick and Carrie were proof that opposites do attract.

Carrie woke up late knowing she could sleep in, since she quit work the week before. With her eyes half open, she slowly wobbled to the bathroom. She reached for her toothbrush and, when she was done brushing, she took a long steamy shower. It made her feel relaxed, as parts of her day and night were uncomfortable due to her pregnancy. She found it amusing that, sometimes, she felt she couldn't recognize herself due to gaining thirty pounds since her first trimester. The heat of the day bothered her, so she spent most of her time indoors.

In a flash, Nick arrived home laden with a decaf caffé Latte with a scone for Carrie and a Grande House Blend for himself. On the way, Nick thought how wonderful his life was with his wife and child-to-be, and not a care in the world. He bounded upstairs, taking three steps at a time, and heard the pounding of the water in the shower.

"Honey, I brought you home something from Starbuck's. I'll leave it downstairs on the kitchen table."

"Okay, I'll be out in a minute," she answered as she slowly turned off the faucet.

Nick restlessly sat at the kitchen table. *Let's see, at 9:33, I'm usually meeting with my team.* Not knowing what to do, he walked out of the French doors leading onto the patio, and oozed himself leisurely into the wrought iron chair under a large umbrella. The day was new, but was already sizzling. The sky showed a bright shade of blue, with the occasional cloud wedged on the horizon. He stood to tilt the umbrella to shade him from the sun. Nick sat and swallowed a sip of coffee. He felt perspiration run down the middle of his back. *Why on earth do I drink this stuff on days like this?* He downed another sip.

With time on his hands, Nick realized that he and Carrie had lived in their home for about a year, and he never walked about the yard other than to mow the lawn. He was without reason to use his new electric hedge clippers, as their shrubs were unhurried to grow. He never actually examined his residence with much thought, except for the day the two decided to make it their home.

Nick and Carrie spent some time outside, but it was on their patio cooking on their gas grill and entertaining friends. But, as far as spending much time outside working on the yard or house, Nick felt swamped with projects at work, so the house could wait. And before Carrie became pregnant, she spent most of her free time setting up house and figuring the outside could wait.

Slouching with his head back following a lazy hawk in the sky, Nick decided to take a stroll and survey their home. He did so in much the proud manner befitting an English squire. But by his fourteenth step, he noticed some scenery he knew was just not right. The edge of the gutter hung well away from the house. Firm-lipped, he shook his head, as this didn't bother him much. But he took note. He sipped his coffee. He walked somewhat slower and, with a squint of his eyes, he noticed several shingles on the garage roof were gone. *That's way up there....* He realized that this wasn't good news but, again, he wasn't overly disturbed. But he took note. Next, he saw that the paint was chipping from the wood siding. *That's probably not too difficult to touch up...It's way up there, though.* Nick took this in stride as well. But he took note. He walked to the other side of the house to a small, wooded door leading to the crawl space. Not knowing what he would find, he pulled it open and the hinge spoke back to him with a screech. Bending down, he slowly stuck his head into the dark, cool and musty space. He heard what sounded like trickling water. Finally his eyes adjusted to the dark space, and Nick spotted a slight leak flowing from one of the joints of a pipe. No longer did he take note on his series of problems. With that tiny flow he began to gush with anger. Still holding on to his coffee cup with one hand, he began to feel and massage the area around the leak thinking that he could miraculously stop the constant stream.

"What the hell is going on here—I don't know what to do about this stuff," Nick hollered knowing no one could hear him as he let off steam.

Still on his knees, he backed his way out of the small passageway and slammed the hatch shut, shaking his head. Directly above him was the living room window, so he reached up to the sill, firmly grabbed its lip and tried to pull himself up. While doing so, like paper mache, part of the sill came off in his hand. Fuming, he tossed the rotten wood to the ground with his coffee cup. Face to face with the dilapidated sill, he began to examine all the boards close to the window and, in disbelief, realized that, under the coat of eggshell white, was eggshell mush.

He looked up and assumed that most of the side of the house needed to be replaced. *I don't like heights—I don't do this kind of thing. Who the hell does?*

At twenty-five, he now knew what his father felt when challenged by his house. But, like most men of his ilk, he proceeded to do the first thing that came to mind. He trotted back inside and found Carrie sitting at the kitchen table enjoying her scone. Out of breath and agitated, he told her in great detail about the problems.

"Thanks for the coffee and scone," she said trying to divert his unbridled anger. "Hold on and get a grip, Nick. I'll take care of it," she said with a stern demeanor. "I know that you don't like heights," she followed with a playful tone in her voice, as she walked to a desk drawer and pulled out the yellow pages. Carrie began at once rooting through the directory to find the right handy man for the job. One, of course, who is not afraid of heights.

"Just go online to find someone. It's faster," Nick said with authority.

"Nick, I got it under control. Sit down and cool off." Carrie said calmly.

Not realizing the difficulty of the situation, they soon understood that finding someone to repair their wall was, by no means, an easy job. Handy men are a selective breed and specific in what they are willing and not willing to repair. She spent an hour on the phone leaving messages or talking with many who told her that the job sounded too small for them or, on the other hand, too big to fit in. By the end of the morning, she uncovered three craftsmen who were willing to visit with them and give them estimates.

The first handy man was to arrive at nine o'clock on the following Monday morning. He never showed. Carrie scratched his name from the list. The second worker honored his appointment the next day and wrote up an estimate. Carrie noticed that Wallace wore a blue oxford shirt and khaki work pants that was a speck too starched and, upon shaking his hand, she wondered if he ever held a hammer in his life.

That evening when Nick got home from work, she told him that the worker showed up on time and he appeared to be professional.

"He had all the right answers as far as materials he would use, length of time it would take him, as well as other work he uncovered and thought we should do at the same time," she told him.

"We'll, honey, that's good. Cancel the third guy and set it up with this man you talked to today." Nick said smugly as if he were in control.

Confidently Carrie responded to Nick. "I don't know. Something about him seemed sketchy. Nope, I don't feel good about him. The third man will be here the day after tomorrow."

Leaving it completely up to Carrie, Nick gave in without any qualms and was fine with her decision.

Pete, the third handy man, came by their house right on time, like the second man, but that's were the similarities ended. Looking spent, he was worn out from a long hot day of rolling out tarpaper on someone's roof in preparation for attaching shingling. His discolored tee shirt was torn in places and his jeans were more black than blue. Pete wore a cap over a mop of blond scruffy hair. Carrie offered him something to drink.

"I don't want to impose, but I would appreciate some water. It doesn't have to be in a fancy bottle—just from the tap is fine."

After Pete gulped the tall glass of water, he asked Carrie to show him the problem. They both walked around to the side of the house. Placing his hands on his hips and leaning squarely on one leg, he scanned the siding. Pete walked close enough to the wall to lightly place the palm of his hand on the boards. He then poked at them with his long slender and dirty finger. He narrowed his eyes and looked up and down at the side of the house. Peering upward he scratched his neck and pursed his lips.

Taking a long deliberative breath he spoke." That's a big job ma'am," he said apologetically. "See, I'm gonna have to pull off some extra boards around the window that I think are rotten, and I'm afraid you've got some damage underneath some of those boards too. Just hope it hasn't gone too far."

Pete wrote up an estimate and gave it to my Carrie. He went on to say, "to do this job right will take some time. You want to make sure the job is done with care, and that it doesn't look like a patch job."

That evening Carrie discussed what Pete told her. She compared the two estimates she got from each of the two handymen.

Like a detective she contrasted the two men. "The first guy's cost for labor is less than Pete's but his materials are almost double what Pete estimated," she told Nick. "There was something a little too slick about that first guy—he was a bit too pressed and perfect for me, I but wanted to fill you in since there is a discrepancy in cost."

Nick asked, "so do you mean to tell me that this Pete guy gave you a higher estimate but you'd rather go with him?"

"Yeah, I'd go with Pete because he stressed the fact that the quality of his work was important and may take longer. That accounts for his higher charge. The other guy, old Wallace, didn't talk about quality at all, and his materials are twice the price of Pete's. Wallace isn't honest." Carrie flatly stated.

Always amazed at his wife's intuitive nature, Nick knew she had to be right.

About a week later, Pete started on the job. As jobs go, this one was uneventful for the first four days. On that fourth and final day of the job, Pete was at the top of his ladder reaching to apply the final stroke of his paintbrush when, without warning, his hammer came loose from his tool belt and careened downward. He heard a thud. The hammer had plunged into their air conditioning unit.

Wide eyed and stunned, Pete jockeyed with jackrabbit speed down the ladder and examined the damage. The claw of the hammer gashed the grill and the pipe that carried the Freon within the unit was leaking. With urgency, Pete ran to the door and called for Carrie. Pete told her of the mishap.

"I'll pay for it all, don't worry about a thing," Pete anguished. "I don't want you to be a day without AC in your condition—I'm just so sorry," he continued. With calmness, she told him not to worry.

"Hang on, hang on. I'll call the air conditioning service number. Think good thoughts…" She learned from her call to the lady at the company that a serviceman was completing a job in the area and that he would be out in the hour.

Two hours later a squatty, younger man, with too much hair bunched on his head, and fresh food stains on his gray uniform, arrived on the scene. Walking to the side of the house where the unit stood, he looked at it and, in a matter of a minute or two, sized up the situation. He spent more time making assumptions than in developing honest appraisal.

"Well, it looks like a nasty gash here. I can have you fixed up in no time. I'm going to have to replace most of the unit, and I'm not so sure how long that's going to take. The machinery alone will be about thirteen or fourteen hundred dollars, and may take up to ten days to get."

"How much? Ten days!" Pete began to feel sick to his stomach.

"How about labor costs? How long will it take you to fix it?" Carrie keeping her cool asked matter-of-factly. "Well, that depends. If I get a good breakfast in me, I could take care of it in short order. If I have a pretty rough go that morning, oh, I don't know—it could take me much longer."

Pete held back an angry response, but Carrie didn't. At a boiling point, she demanded the squatty man leave at once.

Pete worked on keeping calm in the midst of a situation that was bounding out of control. He focused his energy and asked Carrie if she could call two other air conditioning services for other estimates. She amiably agreed. He then asked if she would trust him if she could excuse him for the rest of the day so he could talk to a friend who might be able to help.

"Thanks. I know I have insurance for things like this, but it would hit me hard if I have to file a claim like this. I can't afford more insurance payments. I'll call you later today to see how we can solve this. Thank you." Pete drove off.

That afternoon, Carrie called other services, and was either put on hold indefinitely, or told no one could come out to give her an estimate that day or the next.

Early that evening, before Nick arrived home, Pete called Carrie and asked if a friend of his, who owns a small air conditioning and refrigeration repair service, could come by in the morning and take a look at the problem. Carrie was pleased with Pete's news. Pete offered to pay for a hotel that night, but Carrie declined and told him that they would spend the night at Nick's parents' home.

Very early the next morning, an older black man in an orange rickety pickup truck pulled to the front of the house. On the side of the truck was emblazoned "Virgil Matters" and "I Can Fix This". Pete, in his Nissan pickup, pulled up directly behind him. Carrie and Nick were already there. He was on the front steps working his Blackberry, and she was sitting on the front porch swing.

As soon as Pete's friend opened the door to his truck, he was out like a flash and, instinctively, walked in the direction of the ailing unit. Pete double-timed to catch up with him. In complete silence, Carrie and Nick walked over to where the two stood. Still in silence, Virgil, with the precision of a diamond cutter, reviewed the damaged coils. Then, after some verbal utterances, Virgil raised his head and looked at the three.

"How'd ya do? I'm Virgil Matters and I can fix this. Probably cost three to three hundred and fifty dollars, but it'll be like new. You can trust me."

Virgil's head was full of gray hair, as was his mustache. Quite distinguished looking, he held himself tall, although he was probably only five feet eight inches. His smile was contagious, and he showed it as he told Carrie and Nick the news they were hoping to hear.

Nick spoke up in shock. "You can? Don't you need a good breakfast, order an expensive piece, yank it all apart and sock it to Pete and his insurance company?"

Virgil laughed. "Mister, people usually ask both Pete and me to come back for future jobs and, I might say, we are happy to oblige. See, that's how we make a life."

Nick shook his head and smiled. "I like that—you said that's how you make a life. You didn't say and that's how you make a living."

"You so right, so right. See, my Lord lives in me from my head to my heart to the soles of my feet—so it's easy for me to do what's right feeling that. Some days I have to remind myself of that, but I'm glad I do."

"So you consciously work on it?" Nick was more interested in what Virgil was saying and less about the air conditioner.

Virgil, with warm smiling eyes said, "You know, too, there's something about taking care of each other. It so happens that it comes back to me in some shape or form, and it's pretty good when it does. Oh, yes, sir."

"You're a smart man," Nick said kindly.

"No sir, not really. My mamma taught me to treat everyone and every thing with compassion, and to see no difference between the preacher and the drunk. That's the way. Don't you think?"

When Virgil spoke these words, Nick felt a tingle run through his body, and it wasn't because his cell phone was on "vibrate." Nick looked at Carrie and realized something that she always knew, and something he probably always knew, but was buried somewhere.

Later that evening, when the house began to cool down, and Pete and Virgil were long gone, Nick confided in Carrie.

"People come in and out of each other's lives—some more memorable than others. Pete and Virgil are what it's all about... I mean they use touch instead of tech. I guess the "old schoolers" are a force to be reckoned with. It will come back to them. I'll for sure recommend them whenever I can. You know they connected with me, and they did it face to face. Please remind me when I get too wrapped into the "things" and not people. No texting to get this job done."

With a lilt in her voice, Carrie reconfirmed his sentiments and said, "With this baby on the way, you bet I'll remind you. You know there's no texting an infant—just touching."

Carrie looked lovingly at her husband, realizing that he had an epiphany. Working all day within another world, with people who speak another language, she knew that Pete and Virgil's service, and their love for others, was striking and resonating. Just their simple actions connected with Pete. Heather liked what she witnessed.

***

…you shall love the Lord your God with all your heart, and with all your soul and with all your mind. This is the great and first commandment. And a second is like it, you shall love your neighbor as yourself.
                              – The New Testament, Jesus

Be the change you want to see in the world.
                              – Mahatma Gandhi

I have been to the end of the earth. I have been to the end of the water. I have been to the end of the sky. I have been to the end of the mountains. I have found none that are not my friends.
                              – Navajo

***

Our essence resides in our heart, mind and soul. Jesus asks us to love God with what makes us who we are. This sounds simple. Love your neighbor as yourself. Seems easy enough. What makes it complex are the layers of ego we wrap around ourselves. We are distracted by which we attach ourselves. Unwittingly, we miss out, until we are reminded that we control the change that comes from within. We have a choice, like the Navajo, to find friends at the ends of the earth, at the depths of the sea, upon the peaks of the mountains and beyond the vastness of the sky. It's doable.

***

LISTENING TO

FAMILY

BEGINNINGS

If we have not found heaven within, it is a certainty we will not find it without.

— Henry Miller

Henry's three-thousand-mile sojourn was a trip he needed to take alone. He insisted that Caitlyn, his wife of fifteen years, stay home to take care of their children, Luke and Lucy.

Waking early that day, Henry dressed as if he was going into the office. In typical fashion he had looked through his countless number of suits and chose a dark blue suit with a trace of a red pinstripe that he determined went well with a burgundy silk tie. Traveling was matter of fact, as his numerous business trips were a common occurrence. His overnight bag was always ready. Packed the night before, it was positioned by the front door.

Straightening his tie, and then combing his hair, he saw an unfeeling face in the mirror. In a way, the image was unrecognizable to Henry. His once gleaming gold hair was a few shades darker, speckled with hints of silver. Still a fit and a youthful looking man, Henry felt old and drawn after hearing the news.

Ambition and self are lonely in the company of each other. Blind and deaf by choice, Henry was about Henry. Somewhere along the way, he took a path that was calculated, contrived and costly as his marriage was neither happy nor sad, but was an existence which became a limp appendage of his life. In spite of what he had become, he was loved.

His first flight that morning was on time and although his connecting flight was delayed due to thunderstorms in Charlotte, his long day of travel was uneventful in his mind. Jaded from a decade of steady business travel that took him over the globe, he was now on one trip he took infrequently.

Henry was keenly aware of the many years of his absence from his boyhood home, and it rang in his mind with every mile he drew closer. With little time to waste, once he got off the plane, he headed to the car rental desk. Disturbed they didn't have a full-sized car at his disposal, he reluctantly accepted a smaller substitute. He headed home.

He peered from right to left as he drove from the airport through the city where he spent much of his youth. Much was different along his route. Only the roads home remained the same. Churning thoughts bounced in his head, but he concluded that this was just the way it was. My life is now someplace else.

Like dawn enticing morning light, upon approaching the entrance to his mom and dad's subdivision, he felt a conflicting surge of emotions and thoughts that suddenly thrust him back in time. While the day was overcast, colorless and misty, Mr. Stanford's yard still seemed pristine amid a rainbow of plants and flowers. On the other side the McCaffery's huge house on the corner, claiming two additions, still showed a sliver of a footpath where he, as a kid, would cut through on his way home for his favorite meal of pot roast and potatoes. Henry smiled as he remembered the words "Don't cut through my yard."

But as he drove, he couldn't help but observe the signs of younger families who now lived in the neighborhood. Drumming this moment home, in the adjacent house to his parents' yard, stood a red, white and blue six-foot-tall wooden stork with an announcement of the births, weights, lengths and times of birth of twins.

Pulling up the driveway he stopped the car, turned it off and sat motionless. Absorbing all that bombarded him, without warning, the why he was coming home rocketed to his consciousness.

Henry was coming home to watch his mother die.

Before Henry could assemble his next thought, his father erupted from the house and paced to the car. Seeing all six-feet-four inches of his dad moving toward him, Henry felt happy. His father seemed unchanged. Always sporting longer hair than his contemporaries, he was a barrel of a man on spindly but long legs. "Henry, I was wondering when you'd get here," his dad said robustly. He wrapped his muscular arms around his son's shoulders like a warm blanket. In high, but guarded spirits to see one another, they looked at each other with tears in their eyes.

Henry heard the faintness of upbeat music and didn't know where it was coming from. Paying little attention to his surroundings, but placing his focus on his dad, they sauntered up the long and meandering walkway. "How are Caitlyn and our grandchildren?" Henry gave few details but assured him all was fine as he became preoccupied with the music he heard. It became louder with each step. Climbing the brick stoop, Henry was bewildered as music and laughter emanated from the house. Stepping into the foyer, Henry couldn't believe his eyes. Two dozen people he did not know were sitting and chatting nonstop all throughout the downstairs. Aromas of a medley of foods accompanied by hearty laughter consumed the air. What is going on here? Incensed with his father's demeanor and the order of his house, Henry pushed away from his dad, nearly knocking him off balance.

"Shouldn't you be taking care of her?" he said in a low, harsh tone and worried how he'd come across to the strangers in the house. Not waiting for an answer, Henry with more composure asked, "Dad, what the hell is going on here? Where's Mom?"

"What does it look like?" he asked his son in a quiet and gentle but affirmative manner. "We're celebrating."

Henry was thinking that his parents were out of touch with reality and couldn't believe what he was witnessing. With immense concern and controlled bitterness he continued, "What are you celebrating for crying out loud?"

"Why, our neighbors, Curt and Simone have two new beautiful babies."

Only four weeks earlier, Henry's mom phoned him with devastating news. She divulged to him that she was diagnosed with inoperable cancer that very day of the call. With resolve and with love she told him it was a kind of cancer that goes undetected, and spreads without warning in a short period of time. She told Henry, their only son, that she was given only a month or so to live.

Now numb but beginning to accept the circumstances, Henry said, "I can't believe this. Mom is dying and you're throwing a party? Where is she?"

"She's back in the sun room with the couple and their babies," said his dad and with a growing tone of agitation. He continued with the sense of a command, "now, Henry, don't mess this up for your mom. You may not understand but she was the one who insisted on this party."

Henry sped to his mom's bedside pushing his way to get to her. He didn't know what condition he would find her. As he entered the threshold of where she was, Henry's mom appeared frail and weak. Her actions, though, seemed strong. She was engrossed in conversation with Curt and Simone. As she often did, she used her hands and fingers to punctuate her sentences and Henry caught sight of this, even though she cradled a baby in each of her arms. She didn't know that Henry looked on. Feeble or not, she was vital and alive.

Between sentences, she paused and looked up only to find her son. Her eyes twinkled with spirit much the same way he remembered her when he came home from a summer away when he was sixteen. Henry smiled and, like a timid child, he walked to her and knelt next to her, disturbing no one. He reached out and caressed her soft cheek with the outside of his fingers.

Quietly he asked, "Mother, how are you?"

Difficult to hear her voice, as it was intertwined in the murmur of the room, she answered him with the same selfless tenor as she always did, "I've been waiting for this day. I'm fine. I really am fine."

Her answer sent Henry's feelings in different directions. "What do you mean?"

"Look at these two precious bundles and look at you. I wanted you all by my side, and here you are. Things couldn't be better. Simone and Curt named them for your father and me. Aren't they wonderful?"

Confusion was escalating in Henry's mind, but he nodded and mustered a faint smile. Feeling a tender elbow to his ribs, he looked up and saw his Uncle Bart.

"May I cut in young man?" he quipped. Henry turned back to his mom. Bart was Henry's mother's older brother. He was rather feeble, but managed his way across the crowded room with his walker. Henry was surprised to see him standing there and, fearful he might blow the gigantic bicycle horn that was fastened to his handle, Henry moved aside. As he did, Henry spoke to his mother reassuringly.

"Mom, I'll be back to talk with you in a while," Henry said, not knowing what he would do next. He glanced around the room and found an open seat on the sofa in the family room. He sat, watching the faces in the room. The sounds of the music and the voices sounded more melodic and less threatening. He wondered what they were saying to each other. A moment later, Henry's dad brought him a Budweiser and his patented look of "be patient, son". Henry took the bottle and held it between his legs with both hands. With a lopsided smile, and with thoughts rolling in his head like a pinball game, he continued to sit and stared at the guests.

A man who was a contemporary of his parents came and sat next to Henry. His look was distinctive. His cleanly shaved head had a gleam and his full gray beard was thick. He wore tiny eyeglasses, although his eyes were rather large. It dawned on Henry that this man might be a professor of his twenty-five years earlier. He wore a deep green turtleneck and brown herringbone coat much as his old teacher dressed years before.

Henry thought of speaking to the stranger, but decided to stay tight-lipped. A moment later, with brash enthusiasm, he asked the man, "are you Dr. Zighenhaus?"

"No, I'm afraid I'm not a Doctor. My name is Jack Schmidt; I'm sorry not to be who you want me to be. Please call me Jack."

"You just looked like someone who I once knew."

They sat only another moment when Jack spoke up and said, "I've known your mom for twenty- some years—we sang in the church choir together. She's special, but you know that I'm sure. Knowing her, she probably didn't tell you, but she is like a mom to Simone and Curt." He pointed to the couple and grinned.

He continued what he was saying. "They're only twenty-two or so. Both are orphans, and knew nothing about what they got themselves into; heck your folks helped them buy the place next door." Jack realized that he might be giving too much information. "Oops, I only know this because I introduced them to your folks. For some reason, your mom and dad took hold of them just at a time they needed a hold. Hannah and Big Henry are good, good folks."

Hearing what the man told him, Henry whined, "why is everyone, especially my mom, so happy? I mean she is near death—could be any day."

Jack leaned forward and turned to face Henry directly. "Oh yeah, she's happy and we're happy for her. It's the way she lived her life, boy. You should know—you lived with her and have known her all your darn life." Jack changed his tone and sat back and added, "last Sunday we took her to church. She hadn't been in a few weeks because of setbacks. Gosh, we thought she wasn't going to make it to see today," Jack said, looking around the room, smiling at those passing by. Henry held an eerie feeling and didn't like it that Jack knew something about his mom that he should know.

Jack continued, "You ask me why she's happy, and I think it is obvious. You figure it out, because I'm going to get some of that crab dip over there."

Perhaps a bit less confused, Henry was still mystified. He watched others walk up and talk with his mom. Some were teary-eyed but when they walked away from her, they wore a genuine smile.

About four o'clock Hannah and Big Henry's friends thinned out. The music still played, as his mom didn't want the silence. Some of the women and a few men scurried around the house picking up plastic cups and paper plates. Big Henry was given instructions by a short lady with very tall hair about what casseroles and finger foods were left, and what would last and could be served another day. By now, Henry's coat was off, his tie was loosened and his sleeves were rolled up. He walked out the front door and listlessly sat on the front porch swing waiting for the house to clear. Looking down, he saw a speck of crab dip hardened on his tie.

He said very little, but waved and nodded to the company who walked passed him. The last to leave were Curt, Simone and their sleeping infants. Henry jumped up to help Curt manage the double stroller down the steps, waved good-bye and watched the two walk to the next house. Simone said something to Curt, retraced her step and took a seat next to Henry.

"I just love your mom. She's so good. I hope I can be just like her and I hope, somehow, we can keep her in our lives and in our children's lives."

Tired, Henry said, "what are you talking about? She's dying. Doesn't anyone get it? I came home to see her die. I know she's a good person, but she's flipped out or something. I mean she's throwing a party when, in a few days, we could be burying her. I don't get it—just don't get it."

"Oh, I'm sorry, Henry. I see her in such a different way. Her attitude about life helped me to go on," Simone said with surprise. "I assumed...," she stopped, quietly said goodnight and went home. "I should be running along. It was nice to meet you."

With a sigh, Henry went into the house to find his mom asleep. He sat next to her and prayed. His prayer went from a solemn and formal verse to a more free flow of thoughts about her. In his quiet meditation, he began to hear his thoughts. Introspection in his past escaped him but the moment was new—was alive and warm. His thoughts forced him to smile and, on occasion, he laughed to himself as he gazed with trepidation down at her. She rested in comfort, although he knew her insides were riddled with cancer.

He remembered many times they shared. She read him stories. She fixed his favorite toy truck. She bandaged his knees when he took a spill on the very street outside their door. She shooed away the scary thoughts before he went to bed. Above her on the wall, higher than other pictures hung his framed artwork from the third grade. As he glanced up and saw it displayed above her head, a nourished feeling came over him.

He remembered how she would wait up for him when he was a miserable teenager. He imagined how empty she probably felt, but how inspiring she was to him when he moved many miles away to chase his dream, albeit foreign to him. His life and hers, he was beginning to realize, would always be knotted and inseparable.

Big Henry walked up behind Henry, placed a cold beer bottle on the back of Henry's neck, and grabbed his arm, leading him to the couch. There, they sat.

"I know this is difficult for you. She's your mom. If we didn't throw this party today you'd be coming home to a funeral sooner than expected. She's something, your mother. See, buddy, she lived her life in such a way that, when time came for her to move on, she would be willing and happy to make that next step. No regrets for that lady. She's a class act. I only hope I can be half the person she is when my time comes—yes sir, and it will come... we all die—supposed to. Sometimes folks don't seem to remember that their time will come. Hey, she's joyful—she's ready. Let her know that you are okay."

As this was the first time Henry heard these words, he was struck to his core. Henry began to weep into his hands. In the presence of his father, he felt ashamed and alone until he felt the warmth of his father's embrace.

A few minutes later, Henry regained some composure and said, "Dad, I can understand all that, but I hurt. I've been away so long and, when she needed me most, I'm only here to say good-bye."

Big Henry, with his eyes welling up, pulled back but reached forward, as he had done many times before, and held his son's chin with his large hand. In no uncertain terms, he spoke lovingly to Henry. "What are you talking about, son? You are a part of each other. She's not afraid of death, and she doesn't want anyone to be afraid for her. She knows she is going on to something she deserves."

Henry said nothing, but with the collision of so many emotions that day he tried to understand what his father was telling him.

His father continued, "You saw today how she touched those people. It's been her attitude her whole life. She thinks it, and she does it, again and again, until she gets it right, at least in her mind. But she was going nowhere, if you know what I mean, until she celebrated a birth one more time, and she's wasn't going anywhere until she saw your mug one more time."

Henry mulled over his father's words. He thought about Simone's words. He thought about Jack's words he heard earlier that day. He heard the words from somewhere inside of himself.

At ten o'clock that night, Henry's mom stirred. Henry was sleeping on the couch next to her, but quickly awoke and pulled back the colorful afghan his mother embroidered years before. She called to him and he joined her where she was resting.

"I love you son, thank you for coming."

"I love you too, mommy—don't need to thank me for coming."

"I know you're confused with all of this today, and I'm sorry to bring you that kind of worry, but I assure you that I am fine, and that today could-n't have been better. It was the best day of my life."

"I don't understand how you can call this the best day of your life.

Mom, you are leaving us and we won't see you again."

"Henry, I said this is the best day of my life—not yours. I'm saying I'm ready to take that next step. I wasn't ready until I saw those two babies and, most of all, that I saw you. One reason this is true is because I wanted you to see me happy. I wanted you to see that you need not worry about me and that I am ready. We are not meant to be here for a long time—gosh, wouldn't want to be," she pronounced with a quiet laugh.

"This is not my end. Just like those babes, I will be reborn into something new and beautiful. There's nothing to fear. I hope you, too, will go home with a sense of renewal. You owe it to your beautiful wife and children. I want you to feel ready, every day of your life. Do you know what I mean? My prayer for you is just that."

"Mom, I understand and I am happy that you look at this time in your life this way, but I can't help feeling sad."

"Oh, darling, you can be sad. I'm not saying that, but be sad that you will miss seeing and talking to me. Don't be sad for me. Will you look at Caitlyn with love?

"I will."

"Will you cherish my grandchildren?"

"I really will."

His mother continued, "now, I think you understand why this is the best day of my life—I got my Henry back. We will always be together. I love you."

"I love you, too."

Henry came home to see how his mother lived.

―――――&⧜⧜⧜&―――――

When it is dark enough, you can see the stars.
― Ralph Waldo Emerson

All human beings should try to learn before they die what
they are running from, and to, and why.

– James Thurber

Our life is merely part of our journey. Not it's beginning or its end – just
a part. Life's lessons aren't always clear and answers don't come to us always
when we want them. But when the sky grows dark, shadows prevail and our
footing is not always sure, we need to listen. If we allow hope into our lives,
even in the form of the faintest beam from the glow of the stars, we may
find comfort. We may find the way.

THE FRAGRANCE OF MY FLOWERS

You are never too old to set another goal or to dream a
new dream.

— C.S. Lewis

Happiness depends upon ourselves.

— Aristotle

The morning was fraught with a myriad of possibilities and opportunities, both for Drew and his dad, Gerald.

Beaming rays of the sun bared themselves with intensity but periodically a light breeze whirled in from the north and encouraged Gerald and other neighbors to extend their stint as they toiled outdoors tending to their yards. Like fine smoking tobacco, there was a select mixture of various early blooming flowers, mulches and fertilizers sitting on each occasional waft of air. Each rendition of Colonial style home, from traditional two-story brick to framed saltbox, on this busy street carried its own unique twist and flavor. With a drawn-out blink and a speck of imagination, one could sense they were transplanted to Colonial Williamsburg.

Gerald lived for this kind of moment. The outdoors was sacred. He yearned to spend much of his free time outside, either in the yard or on walks. Making this happen was now easy, as Gerald was retired. He was a CPA for most of his adult life.

Superiors and co-workers alike never knew that Gerald defined himself in other ways than his profession. The company's bottom line wasn't Gerald's bottom line. He never allowed his career to attach itself to his worth. It was merely a means to an end.

A patient and steady man, Gerald, during his many faithful years of dedicated service to two employers, woke early before dawn, dressed conservatively, with the exception of the decade of the seventies, ate a banana and drank a tall glass of orange juice with extra pulp, packed a bologna sandwich with mustard and left the house in the dark.

Once at work, he spent much of his time inside laboring in a cramped, nondescript office of beiges, browns and grays, with pencil behind a desk. He was highly respected by those he worked for and with, but most thought of him as a quiet fellow with a quick smile who kept to himself. Gerald tended to hum while he was at work in his office, or when he walked the halls. Like singing in the shower his humming was spectacular as he walked the stairwells from floor to floor—he never rode the elevator. As dependable as the rotation of the earth, he returned to his family every day at dusk.

Gerald loved his family and always put them first. He knew his children, whether they realized it or not, depended upon him, even though they could never figure out exactly what he did all day long. Pulling down a good salary over the years, Gerald provided more than enough for Peggy and their three children, Drew, Kara, Lizanne and Casey, their sheep dog.

Kara and Lizanne, his "little girls", always caught a ride on his back up to bed. He made up his own songs to sing and stories to tell. They were entranced with his bald head, and would sit on Gerald's shoulders and pretended to give his head a shine while he read the paper in the evening.

Not much of a sportsman, Gerald spent time throwing a baseball with Drew and learning the lineup to his favorite college basketball team. For what he lacked in coaching abilities, he made up by stressing and instilling a sense of fair play and sportsmanship when he spent time with Drew. The children sensed their dad's stability.

Peggy, like Gerald, was steadfast and patient. She relished her time with her children when they were small, and kept her personal feelings hidden during their rambunctious teenage years. Seemingly stern due to her premature gray hair and piercing light blues eyes against her pale skin, the warmth she exuded when she walked in a room dispelled all ill conceived notions that she was unsympathetic or uncompromising. She was nearly as tall as Gerald, and her hair and day-to-day wardrobe were impeccable. Much to the contrary, in the midst of running a hectic but directed household, she always found time to remind others to live their dreams. Kara wanted desperately to be a veterinarian, and Lizanne, always interested in fashion, followed her dream to work in New York City with some of the best designers. Drew worked hard on the football field and received a scholarship to play college football. An injury sidelined him, but he continued his dream as a coach. Peggy didn't stop with her children. Her discussions with Gerald were no different.

Years before his retirement, one early Saturday morning when the sun was bright, Peggy and Gerald finished their breakfast and continued sitting at the kitchen table, as they did most Saturday mornings. She sipped from her mug of coffee and Gerald took long sips of his green tea. They both read the newspaper from front page to back.

"Gerald, put down the paper," Peggy said with authority, "I want to talk to you."

Gerald put the newspaper on his lap and blankly looked at his wife. "Five years from now, you will retire, Gerald. You are a fit sixty now, and the kids are grown and well on their own. Look out that window."

He did so, and smiled. Looking back at her, he tilted his head, waiting for Peggy to continue.

"For blue blazes, get outside and do what you want to do," Peggy said ending her stern message with a smile.

"I've been hearing you for a long time, Peg. The time's probably ripe."

Gerald made an instant decision that took him decades to make. But then and there, he began his plans to spend as much time as he could under the sun with his hands in the soil. He always wanted to tie his life to mother earth but couldn't figure out exactly how to do this. Peg and his children came first.

From that point on, he was a man on a mission. After work and on weekends, Gerald read books and magazine articles, and took classes at the local community college on gardening, horticulture and landscaping. He wanted to transform his quarter acre of Sandy Creek subdivision into something in which he and Peggy would find joy and a sense of peace. Before long, he started in one corner in the yard and moved outward, redesigning and reshaping his environment. His successes, like planting and harvesting his first vegetable garden, inspired him, as did his failures. He had difficulties and problems when installing an irrigation system. Once he realized that connecting piping was one job that didn't connect him to his passion, he knew it was for someone else.

Ten years passed since he started his quest, and now, at the age of seventy, he was somewhat of an expert. He knew his expertise was more what he learned about himself than what he learned about soil nutrients. Outwardly, Gerald worked with his hands, but he knew he was accomplishing more on his inside. Whether his plants thrived or not, he knew his work was vital for his spirit. He didn't realize it years before, but what was important to him was nourishing his soul by linking his actions with energy he derived from nature.

One day, Drew and his wife, Allison, drove up to the front of his parents' house. "That old fool, what is he doing?" Drew mumbled to Allison, as he yanked back the parking brake.

Drew threw open the car door and trotted over to his father. He lashed out and scolded him as if he were talking to a child. "Dad what are you doing? It's hot as hell out here, and you are tilling this soil the old fashion way—with a shovel and a hoe."

Drew scanned the yard and saw a number of tools. They were all tools with neither an electrical cord nor a motor of any sort. Holding in his anger, Drew stayed silent. By this time Allison joined the two, and put her arm around Drew's waist to calm him down.

Allison, a petite young woman with a calming spirit, rounded Drew's rough edges. Drew was a high school football coach who looked like he could still suit up for Friday night's game. His players thought of him as hardnosed, but knew he would always be at their side if they needed him. A large man with closely cropped blonde hair, his athletic tee shirt seemed pressed and tucked neatly in his shorts. His dad seemed to be just about the opposite. Gerald's button-up short sleeved Hawaiian shirt was wrinkled and its tail was flapping in the breeze. His shorts were long and had many pockets full of things he needed as he worked in the yard. A plastic bag in one pocket and a pen knife in the other.

Rather condescendingly, but not intentionally, Drew spoke up. "Dad, I'm sorry, and I know you like it out here, but you're not being too smart about it. I mean, it's hotter than the hinges of Hades and you're working this patch of ground like you were back about... a hundred years. What about the tiller I gave you two years ago?" Drew asked, not waiting for a reply, and pressed on. Pointing to a patch of yard, Drew became testy and he said, "If you run that thing through this area it will turn up the soil in no time and you'll be ready to plant. What you are doing takes so much time—I can't believe Mom lets you do this. Where is she anyway?"

Agitated but calm, Gerald responded. "Hey, wait a minute. You just wait a darn minute. Mom was out here up until thirty minutes before you both got here. Oh yeah, she approves—thank you for your concern. And by the way, you can tell she approves is by looking at her hands. They're as calloused as mine," Gerald said with satisfaction and a smirk.

"My mom has better sense than that."

"What do you mean—better sense than what?"

"Dad, you're seventy. Money's not an issue. Can't you hire someone to do this for you?"

Shaking his head and looking at Allison with disbelief, Gerald wondered how she communicated with his son. "Allison, you know I love you like a daughter. Tell me: is he always so loud and bossy?"

"I prefer to take the fifth on this," she said. Gerald and Allison both laughed at Drew's expense.

"Sorry honey—you know I love you."

Gerald piped up and said, "son, you just don't understand do you? You're my son, and you think that *you* are protecting me from something, but you are doing the opposite."

Drew shook his head in bewilderment.

"What are you talking about? You don't make sense. You should be taking it easy and enjoying your retirement. Yes, your yard is beautiful. You've spent a lot of time out here. It looks like an English garden, but Dad, you've done enough. You don't need to plant any more boxwoods or Japanese maples. As far as vegetables, you should give up planting green beans or cucumbers. You don't need to grow any more peppers—the grocery store is down the street. Enough is enough."

Gerald paused, and then slowly walked over to a tree he planted twenty years earlier. He rested his shovel against its russet and uneven bark. He took off his cap, wiped his forehead and looked down at the roots showing through the surface of the ground.

"Do you remember planting this tree with me when you were about thirteen?"

Automatically Drew regressed. "Yes sir, I do."

"We'll you may also remember this tree germinated as a sapling, and it was precariously nestled right next to the foundation of our house—a place that it couldn't grow and provide shade for anyone."

Drew stood in front of his dad in silence, listening intently.

"Son, I called you from playing basketball in front of the garage and asked you to pull out a shovel and help me move it to a safe place."

"Yeah, Dad, and we would watch it grow. Mom took pictures of us every year in front of it," Drew said fondly.

Gerald thought Drew would understand. He inhaled a deep breath and, as he did, he tasted the flavors of his yard. Each and every inch of his space came together from the junipers, the lilacs, the wispy pines, the thyme, the rosemary and dill. Then there were the flowers—the flowers were his passion. Gerald knew when each bulb was planted and knew when they would burst forth through the soil. He knew what would happen in his yard no matter what time of year it was.

Breaking the calm silence, Gerald began again, "Do you really think that I am preparing this earth, planting seeds, weeding the beds, fertilizing the soil and watering everyday because I don't know that there is a grocery store down the street? Are you following me yet?

Allison ardently shook her head looking at her husband. "Come on, Drew, your dad knows what he's talking about."

Drew didn't listen to her and said, "No, Dad. What I am saying is that you do not need to do all this, and if you want to do this, I wish you'd use your brain. *Use the damn tiller* I gave you and the other tools. You're going to kill yourself."

Knowing he made no headway with his boy, he said sadly and almost inaudibly, "I was killing myself for forty-five years as a CPA; we're all going to die—don't worry about me. I'm living. *Living*, you hear me? He ended on a crescendo.

Gerald walked over to a stone bench in the middle of his garden that he made using odd stones he found, and signaled to Drew and Allison to join him. Next to the bench was a coiled garden hose. Gerald turned the valve and took a sip from the dense gushing stream.

"You want some water?" Gerald asked.

"No, Dad, were fine."

"You look like you could cool down a bit." With that statement, Gerald placed his thumb over the opening, creating a spray, and abruptly sprayed them both.

Allison yelped with surprise and then giggled. "I think I needed that, Dad," she said.

"I know it cooled me off a bit, too," Drew confessed.

"Yeah, man, feels good doesn't it? Something as simple as that…"

They sat down on the stone bench. Thinking of yet another way to express to his son how he felt about his passion, he offered another example. "You know, your mom and I put a great deal of time and love into this place." Do you know what time and love are?"

"C'mon Dad. We know what time and love are."

"You do? What?

"Well, time is… time—twenty four hours in a day, seven days in a week… that kind of thing. As far as love, I love Allison, and I love you, Mom and my family."

"Just what I thought. You don't know what time or love is. I'm also sorry that I never taught you a long time ago. You had some of it partially correct, but you've got to get the whole blooming picture. Time means, well—seconds, minutes, hours, days, weeks, months and years. This is only part of it, but keep it in mind. Now consider love. Love is joy. When you do something from the heart, that *something* that you do cannot harm you. It can only bring you happiness. I'm putting what *time* I have into something that I *love*… something that brings joy."

"Dad, I can't believe you are talking this way. I don't remember you ever talking this way when we were kids. I mean you always told us the rules and what to do—it was clean and it was exact. For crying out loud, you were an accountant. Heck, you're a Republican."

Drew's instance of humor brought a smile to each of them. He then changed his tack.

"Dad, I'm thirty-three and I don't get you. I mean I am trying to make it in life, and what you say sounds like a riddle. Allison and I want a family one day, just like the kind of family you and mom gave me and my sisters."

"That's admirable, son. I want that for you too, if that is what you want. But please do not spend much of your life keeping things in tidy columns, but realize that life is about joy. It's about nourishing your soul. It's so much more than replicating me and your mom or anyone else for that matter."

"Dad, we got off the subject. If you're going to do this kind of work at your age, then you should use the tiller, among the other tools I bought you. You don't need to spend the day in this heat killing yourself."

Gerald, still perplexed with his son, tried yet another way to loosen his son's thinking.

"Drew, let me put it this way. If I use the contraptions you gave me, I would no longer be putting my heart and my soul into what I am doing. I thrive from my doing, and enjoy what it brings me. No gizmo can ever, EVER help change my course. If my soul, my body, or my heart is not part of what I am doing, what you see here is for naught. I will feel no joy. It means nothing. How, then, do you think my vegetables will taste? What will it do to the fragrance of my flowers?

"I don't understand you. You're gonna kill yourself."

———— ∽∾∽ ————

Lord, who art always the same, give that I know myself, give that I know thee.

— St. Augustine

Ask questions from the heart and you will be answered by the heart.

— Omaha

Most folks are about as happy as they make up their minds to be.

— Abraham Lincoln

———— ❧ ————

We are given choices every moment of every day. How do we make our decisions? Through research, by faith alone or a combination? To know oneself, our heart and our soul, is to come closer to our Creator. Look inside and make up your mind.

———— ❧ ————

THE CLAY POT

From naïve simplicity we arrive at more profound simplicity.
– Albert Schweitzer

Simon was the last one through—he made sure of that. In spite of the humidity and heat outside, the place had a cold drabness and emptiness about it. Never before had Simon seen the house, the house he grew up in, look or feel this way. It was an experience that gripped him tightly and rendered him stunned at first. As he stood in the small foyer, he could still hear his oldest sister, Abbey, hollering down at him, bent in half over the flimsy upstairs banister. In unison, a voice from any other part of the house would sound. "Abbey, quit your shrieking and do not lean over that banister, young lady. You'll kill yourself. I mean it. DON'T lean over," their mom would call out.

An assortment and infusion of luscious aromas, wafting from the kitchen that Simon so vividly recalled as a child, burst in his mind, as if he could walk down the hall, turn the corner, and see his mom, with apron, searching in a cabinet for the next spice to add to the beef stew. He thought of her then as a tall woman, impeccably dressed and her hair never out of place. She did it all from her role as a room mother at school to keeping the house spotless. This thought brought a smile to Simon's face as he now knew that she worked tirelessly, and he and his siblings never noticed.

Simon inspected everything and wanted to take a mental snapshot of, not each corner or alcove, but what he remembered to have happened in those places. Deliberately, Simon walked gently as his tennis shoes softly touched the glistening hardwood floors. He noticed a small wound in the floor. He recalled the day he and his brother, John, on that very spot, wrestled in full cowboy dress about three decades earlier. During the stagecoach robbery, a bona fide western brawl broke out; Simon's six-shooter was found underneath the boys, digging into the floor. The dad untangled them, he recollected, and they spent the rest of the beautiful day in their rooms.

Several miles away, Simon and Alicia lived in their home with their two children, little Simon and Thomas. Both were bountifully blonde, like their mom, showing striking green eyes with lengthy lashes like their dad. An average man with sandy hair, Simon was a journalist covering human interest stories in the city in which he always lived. Travels took him far from his home, but something always led him back to his roots. Alicia was born in California, and the two met in college. Happy to pick up stakes, Alicia who grew up with only her dad, found her new home with Simon to be exactly what she always wanted—full of activity and energy.

Rounding into what was their family room, Simon paused as his mind gave him what seemed to be the muffled sounds of the television. For fifty years or so this place sang to him and his family. Here so much history played out. The Korean Conflict, Sputnik, the assignation of J.F.K. and then Bobby and Martin Luther King of the sixties, the Vietnam War, Neil Armstrong, who walked on the moon, the oil crisis of the seventies, Nixon's resignation, double- digit inflation, the hostages in Iran, the "malaise", the Cold War, Reagan, Tom Cruise, cable TV, Desert Storm, personal computers, cell phones and 9/11 and The Simpsons came to Simon's mind as he retraced steps he had taken many times over so many years. These events clutched the attention of Americans while Simon and his family lived in that house. A tinge of guilt came over Simon, as these events seemed inconsequential in light of the events of his family. What was important to him was the upbringing of all four children, who lived nowhere else but in this house until the day they were married.

Nothing dared to be so remarkable about the exterior of this early suburban home. It was hurriedly built during the post-World-War-II era in the forties. Brick and shingling, all painted white, covered the two-story frame. Only black shutters to the side of each window that rattled in the wind, and some wrought iron, dressed up its face. But the house sat guard, with prominence, at the entrance to the subdivision on the corner of the street. A screened-in side porch was fastened to one side, and a chimney on the other. A dogwood tree, a few pine and maple trees peppered the front yard. A few extra dandelions could be found in the assorted grasses of the yard in spring-time, as well as a bare spot or two in the summer. A dusty gravel driveway held tight to one side of the lot, and a sloping ditch framed the opposite side. What was remarkable was found inside.

Simon's parents were pioneers of suburban living, venturing from the large city to establish a new and different sort of life to rear their children. Opportunities in different parts of the county sprang up in the fifties and they wanted to take full advantage. Owning a car was now necessary as well as lawn mowers, rakes, hedge clippers and other yard tools. Many a Saturday, Simon's father could be found laboring in the yard, attempting jobs he never dreamed of doing as a youngster in the inner city, like pruning tree limbs or raking leaves. A cold Kruger beer was always his reward after an exhausting day in the sun. When Simon came of age to help with yard work, he learned the proper way to rake leaves, cut the grass and the art of how to trim shrubs—according to his dad. That was only the beginning of his education.

It seemed simpler then. No, it didn't just seem, in fact it was. Simon's head churned thought after thought. Thinking of his young family and con-trasting his youth and today he thought: we had three TV stations to choose from and a few radios we shared. We didn't know of all the creeps that slogged around in those days. Now, they are daily in the news. We stayed out late in the summer months, and didn't need to develop hand-eye coordi-nation with video games, but played with balls and board games. We inter-acted with real people, rather than with computer-generated people. Not known to Simon, but his brain triggered a mental slap in the face, and he walked onto the backyard patio.

Looking out at the yard, the frames of the clothesline were standing, unattached to each other like the letter T. What looked like sandpaper, the poles were nothing but rust, as was the swing set that was the focal point of many games and imaginary play. On many of those same Saturdays, Simon's mom could be found airing out the house, with all the windows opened wide, to take full advantage of the breezes. Even on a day like this, the scent of Smithfield bacon and fried eggs would float in the air with the fragrance of his mom's lilac bush that enriched most all her senses. She would never snip a sprig for the house, as she wanted nothing that might risk hurting something so beautiful.

Simon walked through the tall grass of the backyard to the dilapidated clothesline and took a seat on an old stump. Looking at the house, more thoughts ricocheted in his mind.

By midmorning, it was usual for his mom to have done three loads of wash. The sheets and pillowcases would flap in the breeze until afternoon, when she sent one of Simon's sisters out to pull them down, fold them and put them in the upstairs hall linen closet. By eleven or so in the morning, she would have already swept and mopped the kitchen and, by this time of the day, she would be pulling out the vacuum cleaner, waking up any of the teenagers brazen enough to still be loafing in bed.

With a sense of purpose, Simon arose and walked back in the house directly into the family room, and sat on the oversized hearth of the brick fireplace. Saturdays were a kid's day for cartoons. He crooked his neck, gazing at all the empty paneled walls

He thought of his kid brother, John, planted in front of the television, watching an episode of the Jetsons, most times with a Twinkie hidden and out of sight, making sure Mom didn't see his booty. Angela could be found in the back yard on a chaise lounge, the ones with the woven plastic straps that made an imprint on your skin, listening to the radio and applying baby oil, hoping for an even tan. He remembered many times she would lie there without budging for anything, that is, until the phone rang in the kitchen.

Simon walked slowly and thought of how things changed over the years but, in a comforting way, really did not. The house was painted, both inside and out, several times over the years, and an addition was built to accommodate their growing family. Not a whole lot of noticeable changes took place other than that. The furniture seemed to stay the same, as if it was bolted to the, always in the same spot. Each chair, table and sofa had a place, and there was no sense disturbing what was right. The kitchen was always a kitchen; it was nothing like kitchens in modern suburbia. No double sinks, indirect lighting or special seating for guests, so they could talk with the hostess during a fancy dinner party. This house had one porcelain sink, an ordinary overhead light, and no seating for guests as they were not permitted in the kitchen while she prepared dinner. They were to be entertained with a drink in the living room.

Poking his head in the dining room, he looked to where his dad would have sat at Thanksgiving, and down the imaginary table to where his mom would be. He closed his eyes and saw a young family sitting at a large table, all feeling like guests in their own home, sporting their Sunday clothes and eating off the good china. An occasional sip of wine was allowed for all, and a toast was always made—the words now forgotten, but the spirit of the event was replete down to the warm and soothing smells of gravy, warm rolls, mashed potatoes and, of course, the turkey. Thanksgiving was special because it was ours—that's all. So were Christmas and birthdays and the first day of school, Simon thought, as he knew that they will be forever inscribed in his mind.

Simon decided he had seen enough. He felt a wave of despondency come over his otherwise contemplative mind-set, as a tear streamed down his unshaven face. He walked to the foyer and decided to take a look in the coat closet. There in the back, obviously missed by everyone, was a small clay pot. Simon was transported at once to a distant memory.

Aside from formal education, his mother and father showed him and his siblings the way in their unassuming daily actions. They were eager to work hard, and took pride in the smallest most seemingly insignificant efforts. They shared all they had.

Looking at that clay pot, Simon couldn't help remember what it meant. When Simon was a cub scout, he visited an Indian reservation. Not knowing what that was at the time, Simon didn't know where was going. He just knew that the Indians were the bad guys. His mom gave him more money than Simon had ever seen, and told him to come home with nothing in his pocket. Simon was to make sure that he brought home Indian-made artifacts. Simon did what she told him and brought home, among other treasures, the clay pot.

He thought about this experience, and knew it was only later that he learned that money was scarce in his home growing up, but they we were rich compared to most native Americans on reservations. She knew not who she helped but most of all she helped me. . .

The clay pot was important in another way. It rested for many years on a small table in the foyer. There Simon's dad would place the things from his pocket when he came home every night. Many times it was filled with change, a piece of candy or a stick of gum. On a rare occasion, he would add a dollar or two. The children knew they were never to touch that clay pot. Once a month, their father would dole out the collected candy to each of them, and the one child, who he deemed helped their mother the most, was allowed to have the contents of the pot.

With the clay pot in his hand, Simon left the house for the last time. He slowly and methodically locked the door walked to his car and drove home. Later that evening, he called his parents where they now lived in a one-bedroom apartment for senior citizens.

"Mom, you told me you'd never move from our home."

"I remember, Simon, that I said that, but it is time for your father and me to move on. We're old and we are tired."

"But this house was our home where we grew up and is a part of our family. So many memories are here," Simon said with a gentle resonance in this voice.

In a slow even manner, Simon's mother said, "memories are not in that house. They are in your heart. You carry your family with you—always. Our house served our needs and our needs, now, are elsewhere, but the lessons we learned are not in a house, in some building. They are in you. Sweetie, I can always call you that. Look inside yourself, and this will help you to live on the outside." After she spoke, Simon said nothing, and she continued, "My sweet Simon, I expect that you will give your children what comes from inside you, as we hope we gave the same to you and your brother and sisters."

She took Simon off guard with her response but, at that moment, Simon was ready to listen. He was ready to refill the clay pot.

———— ✺ ————

A moment's insight is sometimes worth a life's experience.
— Oliver Wendell Holmes

The more you give, the more good things come to you.
— Crow

───── ⊗⊗⊗⊙ ─────

When was your last epiphany? They're not just for the likes of Edison and Einstein. Wrong turns are always the right turns, as it is all in how we deal with the next turn, and the next, and the next....

Have you noticed that you can't tell some people something new? "I already knew that." A courageous spirit is open to newness and light, and ready to receive and share it. Come back to simplicity of thought, as so much may be learned from something so basic.

───── ⊗⊗⊗⊙ ─────

PURPLE MOUNTAIN MAJESTY

After all, if I can't be myself, who can?
— Auntie Mame

Life is too short for men to take it seriously.
— George Bernard Shaw

Kurt graduated from college and moved to a city which he knew very little about, in an apartment with fraternity brothers he knew everything about. Momentum, Kurt would find, could dull the senses and take one further down a road than what might be desirable. But college days were too fresh, and his beer-stained cap still kept the sun out of his eyes so as to disregard them so soon and so completely was not to be. His friends, with all their shortcomings, were true—they were who they were.

Stepping back, his days on campus were genuinely ones of color and animation, as Kurt looked at his time there as one full of learning, both in the classroom and labs, to exploring the good and the bad of being on his own, taking a real first step to adulthood. He always strove to do what he thought was right. He found out that, in a moment, someone who he thought was honest and of substance could be quite the opposite. He knew that he could be happy only if he followed his own conscience. Coming from a rural community, Kurt enjoyed and appreciated the many sides of those he met of the eight thousand inhabitants of his university situated in the mountains.

Kurt and Jenny dated during their last two years of school. "She keeps me grounded," Kurt would say of Jenny. Like a pond free of the slightest ripple, Kurt was clear-minded as he approached his studies, his ambitions, and they were happy in their relationship.

Jenny was a three-year member of a sorority. Vivacious and imaginative, Jenny was a cute girl from North Carolina with shiny auburn hair. She spent considerable time in the library, but found time to be the president of her sorority. Her sisters insisted she was the reason, three years going, that their house was always voted M.A.D.S for "Most Audaciously Decorated Sorority House" during Greek Week.

A strong student, especially his last two years of school, Kurt was offered a job a month before graduation. The couple was ecstatic when they both learned that their search for jobs in the same city panned out the way they wanted. Kurt started with an investment brokerage house, and Jenny worked in the management trainee program at a large regional bank. They spent most of their free time at her new apartment complex, complete with pool, workout facility and clubhouse. They likened it to an extension of college. Jenny lived there with her best girlfriend, Meg.

Kurt and his fraternity brothers Clayton, Ian and Wally, moved into their apartment on a muggy gray day, dodging several thunderstorms. They lived on the third floor in a decaying apartment on a nondescript street. The halls of the building held a stench, the origin of which was undetectable to the four. As was typical of the friends, they spent an inordinate amount of time making a contest of pinpointing the source of the foul presence. Being late for appointments or being sidetracked from what was most important to them, they obsessed for a while about the odor. Worn down by dead ends, they finally gave up a month or so after moving in, and decided to embrace it in all its glory. They likened it to karma. Its presence made them keenly aware that a force as simple as a stink could throw them off course.

Only Kurt was gainfully employed when the four signed the lease, but the three promised that they would not let Kurt down, and would pull their weight. In a matter of a few weeks, the other three were working at jobs so that they could, at the very least, pay their share of the rent and have enough to keep from starving.

With graduation money and help from his dad, Kurt, in that summer of 1987, bought a ramshackle, closet-sized Cape Cod as investment property, never thinking of moving in. The same month, Kurt proposed to Jenny. He felt good that he was moving steadily along with his plans.

On a Tuesday that fall, Kurt and his three buddies were playing a round of golf, and were totally unaware of what they would find out in the clubhouse at the end of eighteen holes. As the four sipped cold Coors, laughing at missed putts and chip shots that went awry, the bartender began waving his hands, directing them to the television that was hanging from the ceiling in one corner.

"Hey guys...guys, listen up," he shouted pointing to the TV.

It was "Black Tuesday". The worst day for the market in years.

Ian joked, "It's the stink... I knew it." The four laughed to varying degrees. Only Kurt worked in the financial industry, so his laughter was forced. Ian worked for a not-for-profit organization, Clayton managed an independent bookstore and Wally was a systems analyst on an army base.

"Yeah, it's the stink alright," Kurt moaned. Kurt would find, in a short time, that his meager and fledging client base became skittish, and his business took a year and a half to rebound.

Life has a way of moving forward, and Kurt and Jenny were married six months after that golf outing. With a new chapter in front of them, they said goodbye to their roommates and moved from their apartments into Kurt's Cape Cod.

Every weekend the first year of their marriage, they went wild, either pulling down needless walls, or painting the ones they left standing. The trim, the doors and, in some cases, the floor, would be transformed to a color. They felt it was exhilarating to experiment, and their house was their pallet. It was just a coat of paint, the two concluded.

Five years went by, and the two were on a solid financial footing. When Jenny delivered their first child, she decided to stay home. They soon found the house was too small, so they renovated it, repainting inside and out with conservative colors that could offend no one and attract potential buyers. In no time, they sold their first home and made a sizeable profit. They were ready to move to a subdivision that suited their growing family and their status.

Kurt and Jenny bought a house three times larger than their Cape Cod. Kurt's client list grew long and old, as he past the "up and comer" status to be considered a solid broker with a keen sense for what was ripe. He enjoyed making money, especially with the news of their second baby on the way.

On occasion, the couple had Kurt's old fraternity brothers over for a Heineken and a steak on the grill. Clayton had recently married and moved up a few notches at work. Ian, too, was married and had three children, and Wally was single, living around the corner from the apartment the four shared years earlier. The three men were in awe of Kurt, as he obviously was financially successful. They looked at the wealth and the possessions that he and Jenny acquired and felt that things were different beyond the obvious.

"No stink here," said Ian. "I think Wally has it since he lives so close to our old place. Have any of you guys been back to that building?"

"Can't say that I have," said Clayton.

"Nope," Kurt said with a longing tone. "I think I'd like to go back just to see if the stink is still there."

They all laughed. An hour later, they said their good-byes.

After the three left the house they began to talk as they slowly walked to their cars.

"They seem different. I mean they're still the same deep down. It's hard to pinpoint what's changed," said Ian.

"Yeah, I know what you mean. I know we all change, so I don't have a problem with guys moving on," Wally said struggling with what he felt.

"I don't care about their money. I care that they seem to me that all their life has been sucked out of their bodies. Did you see their eyes? They're getting creepy. They are as bland as the beige on their walls, and as boring as the symmetry of their furniture in all their rooms—their house looks like a furniture ad," Clayton said as the others shook their heads with affirmation.

"The only time Kurt seemed to be himself was when we talked about the apartment," Ian said with concern.

A year or so after that visit, and when their second child turned three, Jenny and Kurt began to feel the itch to move. The house they were living in became merely adequate and the schools were not as new as those in the latest subdivision where woods once grew. They decided to put their house on the market and look for a house in Bottoms Stream.

They found the house that they thought they always wanted. They visited the schools and they thought they were in paradise. The house they decided to buy was on a desirable street, where each home was dropped on a tiny lot, but with plenty of flowering trees meticulously arranged like a sophisticated office park. These houses had various floor plans to shake it up somewhat, and the neighborhood teemed with plenty of white, off-white, gray, taupe and beige houses.

Their neighborhood homeowners' association was strict in regard to the prescribed agreed-upon tenets that the board regulated. There was a high expectation and a disturbing fine imposed by the association for all residents not conforming. Very important rules were voted on, such as the maximum height of shrubs and style of tool sheds allowed to each resident. Fence designs had to be presented to the board for approval, and the approved holiday decorations were listed on the association website. This was all spelled out on the website and in the monthly newsletter.

The neighborhood had about three hundred and fifty homes, none smaller than five bedrooms, and a bonus room. They were arranged on a matrix of streets, lanes and courts in such a fashion as to create a web discouraging the garden variety of unwanted house burglar. Unfortunately, it didn't keep high-school-age boys from breaking into garages, looking for beer in the second fridge.

The many neighbors from all over the country made up this community, as the neighborhood was full of white-collar industries that moved to the area, transferring employees in and out at will. This hodgepodge of humanity watched out for one another. Sometimes watching out became merely watching. But it was a community of good, well-intentioned citizens.

It was quite common to see young boys, and the occasional girl, playing touch football in the yards. The usual victory dance after a touchdown was thrown and the argumentative ten-year-old, high-pitched voices shrieking as they refereed themselves, were part of the experience. Couples spent time walking their canine children with a leash in one hand and a plastic Wal-Mart bag, or a yellow newspaper bag in the other, to ensure they were being respectful neighbors. Regardless of ethnicity, here were an abundance of blonde wives and plenty of "Titlist" brand husbands.

The yards were spectacular. Bradford pear trees budded first with their white flowers in April. Azaleas blossomed each May and then came the iris and other flowers in June and July. Crepe myrtles had their day in August, and many other colors followed well into the fall, ending with mums in October. Where the flowers bowed out in autumn, the leaves of many trees took over. These were the only true colors of the neighborhood. Everyone seemed happy—and alike. At least on the outside, they all seemed the same.

Kurt and Jenny, like many, wanted and had, two children. As if it could have been arranged, their son came first, and then their daughter. Grayson was a regular in the neighborhood football game, among other activities like "manhunt" and other forms of hide-and-go-seek games. There were many playmates for Gray and little Lilly. While Gray was at play with other children on the street, Kurt and Jenny strapped Lilly in the stroller and spent time together on walks. Like their neighbors, with their Labrador retriever Shamus, they walked the circuit. A year earlier, when they first moved in, they decided to buy an SUV like others in the subdivision. They were like most others, and had their share of cell phones, personal computers and other "can't live without it" technological paraphernalia. Kurt and Jenny had arrived—they were a couple for the new millennium—the family of the '00's.

During their walks in the neighborhood, Kurt and Jenny would stop and chat with neighbors. Most times the conversations would revolve around the goings on of the community. Most conversations were mind-dulling.

During one particular walk, Kurt and Jenny commented on their neighbors of all shapes and sizes, all decked out in expensive running shoes and outfits, presumably to lessen the horrors of air resistance as they ran. Like an IV, they all had wires attached to their arms, flowing up and inserting music into their head. Jenny would was amused at the spandex-clad runners.

"You know, Kurt, they look ridiculous. When we were growing up, men wouldn't be caught dead with all that stuff. They would just put on some old shorts and a tee shirt and run. Everything is so precise and charged up. That runner guy was in his own world listening to music and flashing across the neighborhood like a rainbow on legs."

Kurt laughed, but stopped short and thought of how they too enjoyed many of the possessions they had acquired. *Huh... I guess we can't look back.*

As they marched on, they stopped to talk to the Fennels, who were tending their flower garden. Mrs. Fennel was always a top contender for a blue ribbon during garden week. That particular day, when Kurt and Jenny stopped to talk, the Fennels informed them that the Carters, two doors down, had a backyard party the week before that lasted well into the morning hours. The Fennels also informed Kurt and Jenny that the Perkins's house was now on the market because their marriage was on the rocks. All of a sudden, a terrible hollow version of Beethoven's "Ode to Joy" came from nowhere. Without excusing herself, Mrs. Fennel pulled off her flower-designed gardening glove, reached into her large apron-like tunic and pulled out her cell phone. "Oh Darcy, I've been waiting for your call. Did you know that...?" After another three seconds of listening to Mrs. Fennel talking into her phone, Kurt nudged Jenny and they managed to bid adieu and went on their merry way.

"You know, Kurt, we've lived here a year, and we know more about the Carters and the Perkinses than we do about the Fennels, and that's who we talk to all the time."

"Yeah, honey, and I don't even know who the Perkinses are. Anyway, you're right. I think she hides behind her garden because she hasn't got anything else to share about herself."

"...she hides behind her cell phone too," Jenny said with contempt.

Continuing down the street, they veered down the next court. It wasn't long until they ran into Mrs. Weedameyer, who was coming toward them. She was accompanied by her Dalmatian, Midge. Kurt was worried that a conversation would ensue and, sure enough, one did. She told Kurt and Jenny that her next door neighbor was building a fence between their properties, and she was livid. She just couldn't believe their nerve. Jenny did a great job of showing interest and gave Mrs. Weedameyer the proper number of head nods and uh huhs. The dogs got into a barking episode, which was fuel to close down the conversation. Relieved to be free, Kurt and Jenny nodded and waved as they moved on.

They hadn't walked ten paces when Kurt said, "Look around, there are fences and walls everywhere. When you think about it, they're like little fiefdoms keeping all the unwelcome out."

And went on home—exhausted.

That night after dinner, with precision, Kurt and Jenny brought up the same topic for conversation as if it were scripted.

"You know Jenny, this place where we live is fake… on top of that, it's been zapped of real color and life. People don't know one another. They think they do and they make up stories to tell others. We know our neighbors through translators, for crying out loud. They add the color—the pizzazz to an otherwise ho-hum existence. People translate," he said forcing a smile.

Jenny spoke up. "You're right about that. We live in the same neighborhood, our kids go to the same schools, and we see the same people and we don't know each other. The essences of our lives are hidden behind lovely houses and curb appeal. What really comes out is drab or neutral at best. I mean we know their names, the house they live in, and only the stories we hear. But, we don't, in truth, know much about them, or what goes on behind their front doors."

"I may be the worst offender, but people don't know each other; they really don't want to. They live for their stuff—technology is their personal baby sitter. Lifeless technology is really the fence between people and they accept it—I ACCEPT IT. Hell, I know people who'd I'd rather email on everything rather than talk to them."

Jenny added, getting a bit steamed up, "people depend on technology to project their personality—it's crazy. I know the bar has been raised, so to speak, but we still need to be people first, instead of robots," Jenny added.

Unlike Kurt's current modus operandi, his actions retreated to a different day, as Kurt jumped from his chair and lightheartedly paced the kitchen, flailing his arms with a dance step periodically placed, he spoke up. "You're right. Well, we only know their yards. You know the grass is spectacular; the Hansons' walkway was repaved and that kind of stuff. We don't really know them and the thing is, they don't know us nor do they want to know us."

The two laughed as they sized up their neighbors but, just as quickly as their laugh came, so did the subsequent bitter silence.

"It's kind of scary," Kurt continued.

"What do you mean—scary?" Jenny asked.

"We have become what we have always despised," Kurt said. "Look at us. We try really hard to fit in, and we've been doing it for a good ten years now.

With a sigh, Jenny's attitude was deflated as she felt the same epiphany as her husband. "I hate to say it but I agree," she said.

"Okay, I'm gonna start by emptying my pocket." Like a summer storm that hits at once, he pulled his cell phone out of his pocket and placed it on the kitchen table. Next, he added his Blackberry, followed by his iPod. He placed his keys with the automatic door locks and alarm system that was on the key chain on the table. Like a madman, he left the room only reentering in a moment with six different remotes for a variety of luxuries. He placed them on the table. He left again and, to Jenny's delight and amusement, he was back in no time with three laptops. He then made a trip to the garage and loaded the table with a number of tools with electronic features and the garage door opener. Nearly out of breath, and with emphasis, he plunked the alarm system key pad on the table.

"Jen, here's the alarm system that protects all our possessions—I know it protects us too, but we didn't think about getting one of these things until we weighted ourselves with possessions. This pile of stuff is just the tip of the iceberg." He concluded plopping himself into a chair to Jenny's applause.

"Kurt, maybe we're jumping to conclusions. It may be that nobody has time anymore to really be who they truly are, and all this stuff becomes a crutch."

"Maybe. But I think it is more than that. Maybe everyone is afraid to let others know who they truly are because they think buying stuff and keeping to themselves protects them from making friends. We all look the same in suburbia, but we aren't the same. We cheat ourselves by the way we live. We just try to blend in so that we all don't become fodder for idle conversation. But it doesn't work. The folks out there don't know what goes on, so they make it up or embellish it."

"I wish people knew everyone's true colors and stopped being so afraid. They whitewash their own lives, and use a wide spectrum of colors for others. Kurt, you are so right. We have become as beige as the rest of them. By being more "connected", I think we are less connected. People don't know each other."

"Jenny, you're right. You know, you've given me an idea."

At that moment, Kurt walked over to Lily's box of 64 Crayola Crayons, picked it up and walked over to Jenny.

"Jenny, you do the honors. I'll hold the box and you close your eyes and pick a color. Whatever color you pick, we'll use to paint our house."

Being the idealist, and without looking, Jenny reached into the box and pulled out a color.

"Great choice my dear—Crayola is getting so creative. I'll call the painters tomorrow and ask them to match this one you picked out.

"We'll, what did I pick?"

"Purple Mountain Majesty."

As far as the inside—let's get rid of these drab walls. Let's paint it like that old little house we owned twenty years ago. How 'bout I give Ian, Clayton and Wally a call and see if they'll help. I'll tempt them with a Coors Light. We'll get this "stink" out of here."

———

To be nobody but yourself in a world which is doing its best to make you everybody else, means to fight the hardest human battle ever and to never stop fighting.
— E.E. Cummings

Don't be consistent, but be simply true.
— Oliver Wendell Holmes

———

Are you true to yourself? More people wear a false nose with attached mustache and glasses than you would think.

———

LISTENING TO
CHILDREN

CIRCUS AND LITTLE GIRLS

Nature's first green is gold,
Her hardest hue to hold.
Her early leaf's a flower;
But only so an hour.
Then leaf subsides to leaf.
So Eden sank to grief,
So dawn goes down to day.
Nothing gold can stay.
  – Robert Frost, "Nothing Gold Can Stay"

Although his vision was fine, Donald was losing his sight. He saw nothing as new, even if it were so. His vision was near perfect when seeing what he wanted to see, as his sights on himself were clear. But he became infected with what most folks suffer from by the time they are forty—some start earlier. He developed a case of the "been there, done that" syndrome. Donald was in a rut and he didn't know it.

Many mornings, he looked in the mirror and he knew he saw someone different than the Donald of two decades earlier. His once-lanky frame, nearing six five now, had plenty of cushion. He hadn't seen his abs in years and all the hair that was left on his head was gray. His crow's feet begot crow's feet. Although too young for hair to grow from his ears, he was a prime candidate. Donald saw these changes, but he was oblivious to the other change that slowly enveloped deep inside him over time. Unlike the loss of desirable hair, and then the arrival of those follicles showing up in the wrong places, this internal evolution could be reversed.

Donald worked as a civil engineer, and managed to leave the stress of his job at work. He loved Libby, his second wife of twelve years and their four girls: the six-year-old twins they had together, and one teenager each from their previous marriages. Not much of an outdoorsman, he enjoyed the comforts of home and looked forward to being there with all his girls. But when a basketball or football game was televised, which was constant due to the availability of more than one hundred cable stations, he was front and center.

Tall and thin, Libby was a dental hygienist. Her family had the whitest, plaque-free teeth in the neighborhood. She enjoyed her job as she could choose her own hours: hygienists were in great demand in their small community. Because of her favorable situation she spent considerable time with their girls.

It was Friday. The week seemed to have two Mondays, and ending it was fine by Libby. After Libby met her two youngest at the bus stop and walked them home for a snack, little Renée and Rebecca watched TV. Their attention was captured by a television commercial advertising the arrival of this year's edition of the circus. In fact, all afternoon, commercials blitzed the area. They knew little about the circus other than fanciful books and what mom told them.

"Momma, can we go to the circus? I'd like to go because it is actually the greatest show on earth and it is coming *here*," Renée sparkled with excitement.

"Yeah, they got lions and clowns," Rebecca added with a huge smile and a tilt of the head, thinking that would clinch the deal.

Renée whispered with alarm, "you know, Becca, I'm a scared of clowns—but I'm okay if they're there."

Their imagination was vivid, and they displayed bubbly energy and excitement about the notion of going to the circus.

"Girls, we will see. I'll ask daddy tonight after we take Katie and Courtney to the mall." Libby knew Donald didn't like the circus. He thought it was a waste of time and the cost was ridiculous. Libby sensed the girls knew that, if she brought their dad into the scenario, they might not go. She wondered how she would finesse this one.

Donald loved Fridays, and today there was even more to love about it. Although the scrawny trees in the neighborhood appeared lifeless, without a bud to be seen, that afternoon, the sky was clear and as blue as tropical waters. The air was oddly warm, and a southwest breeze caressed those who shed their coats for this reprieve.

Headed home early, Donald stopped by Food Lion for Budweiser and steaks. While waiting in the checkout line, he inspected the thick hunk of marbled red beef behind the clear plastic. He was happy with his choice as, in his mind, he could taste it.

Once home, he threw his bounty on the kitchen table, jogged upstairs, pulled off his gray slacks and official black company polo shirt, replacing them with a faded red tee shirt bought at Myrtle Beach eight years earlier, and pulled on his favorite and crumpled olive shorts.

"Libby, Libby—anyone home?" No answer. "Hey Libby—yoo-hoo!" *I guess they're out somewhere.*

Slipping his size thirteen feet into his flip-flops, he headed to the back deck to fire up his gas grill. While it was heating up, Donald went into the family room and flipped the switch of his stereo. Rummaging through a stack of CDs, he came across what he was looking for and popped it into his stereo. He had several speakers rigged outside just for times like this. *Ah, a little Buffet—can't beat it*, he thought. He grabbed a few beers, headed out to the deck and planted himself in a huge overstuffed outdoor swivel chair.

"What's this? Even a drip of sweat," he muttered touching his forehead. "Cold weather is on its way out and I couldn't be happier."

As he downed his last swig of beer from his first bottle, Libby seemed to appear from nowhere.

Poking her head out of the sliding glass door Libby called out, "what are you doing, Donald? Don't you remember that we promised Katie and Courtney that we would drop them at the mall for a movie?"

No answer from Donald. His mouth opened slightly.

"While we were at the mall, we were going to check out a few things for Katie's birthday. Remember?"

Still no answer. Donald's mouth opened more and hung there motionless.

Libby beginning to feel agitated, shook her head in disgust and mumbled, "Donald, sometimes you don't think, or you think of only what suits you." She walked away.

"Oh hell," Donald grumbled to himself. He opened another beer.

Donald grilled his steak and ate alone. Somehow it tasted better in the checkout aisle. He polished off a few more beers, and grew tired of the evening that he thought would be riddled with great potential. Libby and the girls left for an extended trip to the mall. Sitting in his big chair, alone, he had ample time to think. He knew this wasn't the first time that he assumed everyone would stop what they were doing for him. *This wasn't me when Libby and I met, but this was me two years earlier when I got a divorce from my first wife.*

When Donald awoke the next morning, he hoped for a better day. He looked out the window and saw rain with no visible sign of clearing. A shiver came over him as he walked to the bathroom. Donald was amazed how so much could change in what seemed to be an instant.

Downstairs Becca and Renée were playing with Barbies and watching shows on Nickelodeon. Libby was clanking pans in the kitchen. Columbian coffee brewing, and the spattering sounds of bacon frying, managed to cut the cold morning with a sense of warmth. Saying nothing, Donald pulled a large coffee mug from the dishwasher, poured his coffee and sat on a stool at the counter facing Libby. He cupped his large hands around the top of the mug and looked at the extra black liquid emitting swirls of steam running up against his unshaven face.

"I'm sorry. I wasn't thinking again," he said with sincerity.

Libby turned to him and tenderly smiled, "Let's just forget it."

The television was louder than normal and, instead of Donald's usual manner of firmly telling the children to turn down the volume, he said nothing. Libby noticed it, and the girls heard it clearly, but Donald was oblivious to a commercial plugging the circus. As Libby and Donald started to talk about the day ahead, Renée and Becca ran into the kitchen.

"We just saw another commercial," blurted Renée.

"Did you ask, Momma?" the girls gleefully said in unison.

"No, but thanks for reminding me. You all run on in the other room and I'll call you when breakfast is ready."

"But Momma…"

"Now say, 'yes ma'am' and I'll call you for breakfast in a minute."

"Yes ma'am," they said melodically and marched to the other room.

"What's going on? Ask me what?" Donald asked.

"The girls and I want to go to the circus, wouldn't you like to go?" But Donald knew she wasn't asking a question.

"What day are we talking about?" Donald asked knowing he was risking blowing it by not saying "yes" right away.

"Next Sunday evening is the only time we can go as a family—and I want everyone to be able to go; even Courtney and Katie."

Donald knew three things for sure. First, he hated the circus; second, the NCAA basketball tournament championship was scheduled at that time and, third, he knew what his answer should be.

"I think that would be great. I'd love to go," Donald replied and continued. "I mean parents, children and the circus come together like going to school in the fall, spring break and summer vacations. And since Barnum met Bailey, the circus has had weird clowns, people hurling themselves from platform to platform wearing sparkly tights. And then there are those feisty dogs; now how could anyone wonder? All this with aggravated tigers, skinny tightrope walkers and stinky elephants." Donald knew he answered correctly, but also knew he went on too long and what he thought was funny fell with a thud.

Donald was in for a moment he didn't expect. They called the girls in the kitchen and Libby asked Donald to give the girls the good news. Just telling them that they were going to the circus was a reason for the girls to celebrate. Clasping their hands together, jumping in the air and screaming with marvelous smiles created a response Donald wasn't ready for. He knew they would be elated, but it was like he just told them that he was lying all along, and that ice cream and candy are really good for them, and they better get used to eating it for breakfast, lunch and dinner.

Their older kids, on the other hand, who were fourteen and fifteen, didn't respond with the same energy to his news. Donald went from being the best dad in the next five subdivisions to that of a prison guard ready to cuff their ankles to transport them to a chain gang. The older girls were not happy.

Ever since that Friday the week before, each day was unseasonably cold, as Donald no longer had the occasion to wear his shorts and flip-flops. These subtle but certain events gave Donald cause for introspection.

The big day arrived.

"What's taking so long? Isn't it time to go yet?" Becca gushed with questions.

"Can we go early? Are the lions in cages? Don't let the clowns come too close…" said Renée.

The excitement lasted all day. Shortly after a having pizza, all six of them bundled up on a cool misty Sunday afternoon, left the warmth and comfort of their home on their quiet cul-de-sac, hit the highway and traveled downtown to see the circus. Donald wisely put the NCAA tournament out of his mind, and was determined to be the kind of dad his girls deserved.

As they tooled down the highway, the little girls asked why they weren't going to a big tent. This was only the first of many questions that both Donald and Libby couldn't answer. Donald and Libby glanced at each other with a sense of contentment underscored by quiet laughter, as they both began to realize the beauty in the girls' naïveté, knowing that one day it would diminish. In particular, this pushed Donald to a ponderous mood. Donald knew that answers didn't matter, anyway, as the excitement of the afternoon was all they needed.

Parking in a massive garage was exciting—so many cars. Walking a few blocks up to the city's arena, Becca and Renée were in awe of the colossal building. "Is the tent in there?" Becca quietly asked her dad.

Rows and rows of seats filled the building and, looking down to the circus rings then up to the ropes and nets and light, the girls were awestruck. After they found their seats, and before the show began, more questions poured from their mouths. Bug-eyed, the girls saw concessionaires hauling gigantic levels of goodies from toys to treats. Katie and Courtney told their dad how fascinated they were to see how thrilled and ecstatic their sisters were, as the little ones bellowed out one thought after another. With anticipation, their tiny fingers pointed to the high wire. Becca laughed at the sight of clowns flouncing through the stands, as Renée buried her head in Donald's stomach and, peering up from time to time, trying not to let the others see her repressed smile.

Donald was stunned and speechless by such natural and unadulterated excitement. As fast as synapses can travel, Donald was brought to a point in time when he last went to the circus. *Of course—he forgot how to see it.* Until that point, Donald's memory had been clogged. Consumed with both the important and or not-so-important events over the years and other malign thoughts that distanced himself from who he truly was, was the source of Donald's self-centeredness.

As the music boomed the ringmaster sang while the glittering parade began. Donald saw children all around him beam at the sights. The rich pallet of colors, the flittering flecks of confetti, the rainbow of floodlights and the whopping booms of human cannonballs added a roar of anticipation and exhilaration. He was tickled to see his girls take it all in. Donald was so entranced at the sight of his daughters that he missed the show before him, but saw something so breathtaking beside him. *This was the first time they ever saw, touched, heard, tasted and smelled the circus.* From the cotton candy to the stink of the elephants and the precision of the acrobats, they drank it in with zest.

On the way home, everyone talked at once and shared what each liked most. However, they didn't like the smell of the elephants as they paraded by them. Halfway home, just as if a switch was turned, it was now quiet as the two smallest in the family were fast asleep.

"You know, for two hours they experienced something that was completely and purely new, and were fully aware of their senses—gosh, most times adults miss so much because they are so strung out," Donald rambled.

"Honey, tell me about it."

They laughed with such heart, they nearly work the girls.

When they pulled into their driveway and parked, with calm and silence Donald opened the mini van doors and walked around the side of the van. Their oldest children began to file out. Not wanting to go in the first place, they gave their parents a look and a smile telling them they were pleased to be a part of yet another family odyssey. They said good night and went up to bed.

With a proud smile, Donald and Libby looked back at their sleeping girls. Renée clutched her new clown doll, and little Becca's head was tilted and leaning on a twirling light-up toy. Dislodging her from the toy, risking hitting the trigger, Donald safely pulled it away. Like it was second nature, Donald and Libby unbuckled the girls' car seats with care, carried them up to their beds and somehow got them in their pajamas; the pink ones with flowers that they liked, without waking them. They tucked them in and, knowing the nights of these routines were numbered, Libby and Donald glowed just looking at them still and quiet—energy at rest. It was a picture they seldom saw. Donald motioned to Libby that he would follow her in just a moment. He stood looking over them thinking of their boundless spirit and curiosity. He looked at their tender skin faintly illuminated by a soft nightlight and the beams of the moon that evaded the curtains. Somehow, in this darkened room full of shadows cast from stuffed bunnies and tea sets on shelves, he saw things cleanly and clearly. Remembering six years earlier, Donald saw them take their first breath as they held their eyes tightly shut. Maybe they didn't realize it but they saw their dad take a new breath with his eyes wide open. *It felt good to finally see.*

For an evening, Donald unwittingly pried himself away from the shackles of the world's idiocies and self-absorption to see what was beautiful. The beauty their children showed him gave him a lesson that he would not forget. *I forget what it's like to experience as children do for the very first time. Huh... it's not bad to be a beginner—always.*

He tiptoed downstairs, kicked off his shoes and sat next to Libby on the sofa. It was about eleven o'clock and Donald turned on the news.

"Why in hell did I do that?" Donald asked himself. Without another thought he clicked the off button on the remote.

Libby spoke up, "I am so glad you did that. Habits are difficult to break sometimes. Can we just savor our evening a few minutes longer?"

"I'm with you on that one."

———— ❦ ————

And all the loveliest things that there be
Come simply, so it seems to me.
                    — Edna St. Vincent Millay

No matter what you've done for yourself or for humanity,
if you can't look back on having given love and attention
to your own family, what have you really accomplished?
                    — Lee Iacocca

———— ≈∞≈ ————

Most of us don't see nor feel the power children possess. If we did, we would be more interested in what goes into them then what goes into our electronic gadgets.

If we could only value the moment as does a child, or respond to life's treasures with the excitement of seeing them for the first time, we would begin to feel that power. I know this first hand. My daughter of eight, just this moment, interrupted my writing to show me her patriotic red, white and blue potholder she just proudly completed.

———— ≈∞≈ ————

A YOUNG AMERICAN AUTHOR

If we don't turn around, we just may get where we're going.
                                      – Native American saying

Where is the knowledge that is lost in information?
Where is the wisdom that is lost in knowledge?
                                      – T.S. Eliot

Like most days after school, Eli rode clanking yellow bus number forty-seven. The windows were wide open, and wafts of flowering trees trailed in and out, working overtime to camouflage the odor of the overly active children. The bus zipped through the neighborhoods, rattling from inside out at each stop. With his eyes fixed to the words on the frayed pages of his paperback, oversized and self-important fifth graders, sitting both in front and behind him, began to taunt Eli. Paying little attention to the obnoxious affront, he kept reading the words, trying to make sense of them in the middle of mayhem.

Slight of build, and a few inches taller than the others in his class, Eli was quiet and thoughtful; he was always a gentleman. Fearful of little, Eli was a dreamer. He was endearing, with an easy smile, and his dirty blond hair fashioned a cowlick to his right side, no matter what his mother would dab on his head. Always second or third to be chosen by team captains at recess, he was faster and more elusive than most during those games of tag and other games. The others found it daunting to catch, tag or corner Eli as he seemed to be able to will himself to safety. A friend of many, no one could be considered his shadow, or he a shadow to anyone else. Arithmetic was unpleasant for Eli. Science and history were fine. Art and music were fun, and writing and reading were his forte.

Eli loved to read. Reading on his own, by summer prior to kindergarten, he read everything from Harry Potter books to the Goosebumps and the Animorph series. His classmates were tempted to tease Eli, but didn't dare as he was a skillful runner, and his weaknesses could be overlooked. Eli, however, was not immune from the fifth-grade boys.

His bus ride home, many times, was unpleasant at best.

"What a wussie…," Purvis, a fifth grade boy jeered. "Don't you know books are for girls, especially books like that one?" said another fifth grader. Enduring their harangue was grueling but he remembered his mother's words that encouraged him to ignore the feeding of insatiable "animals". From the corner of his eye, Eli was glad to see that his stop was coming near, so he could escape the rancor of the aimless passengers. Much to Eli's astonishment, the ringleader of the group would continue following him.

As Eli bounded down the steps of the bus, he felt a hot putrid breath spewing on the back of his neck. He heard a mumble in his ear. "You better start running, wimp." Heeding the warning, Eli took off like a startled jackrabbit, being weighed down only by his back-pack. Daring not to drop his belongings, Eli decided to lose his marauder by outsmarting him. Rounding a neighbor's house, he hid in the boxwoods. Purvis, out of breath, snooped around the shrubs and, like a hunting dog, picked up Eli's scent. Nowhere to go, Eli was cornered. Purvis grabbed Eli's arm and yanked him with force to the driveway.

"So, you thought you could outrun me? I'm not a fourth grade punk, you know, dweeb."

"No, you're a fifth grade punk…!"

Shocked that Eli countered that way, Purvis pushed him to the rough surface and pinned Eli down on the pebbled driveway. Ruthlessly, the boy's knee rested squarely on Eli's cheek, stifling any utterance he could drum forth. The boy grabbed the book out of the fourth-grader's hand, tore it in half and heaved it to the driveway. "So you think I'm a punk, do ya?"

All at once, the side door to the house opened. There stood a tall white-headed man, with a long walking stick that was knotted and gnarly at one end. He waved it like a sorcerer and startled Purvis. Dumbfounded, he hopped to his feet and fled. Eli gently caressed the side of his face and wiped lingering pebbles from his cheek, leaving a red and pocked temporary imprint. A deeper imprint within would last.

The old man helped Eli to his feet and dusted him off.

With a resonant and soothing voice the old man said, "You okay, little man?"

"I guess so," Eli muttered, looking down to the place where he was accosted.

"Would you like me to call your mum?" The man asked.

Holding back a tear, Eli found a way to answer. "No... no, I'm fine."

The old man crouched down and retrieved the first half of the book and read its cover. "Ah, *Letters to Children*. Aren't you a bit young to be reading C.S. Lewis?"

"NO! I mean... no sir. I've been reading a long time, and I've finished all the little kid books. One day I'm going to be a writer too... and be published—probably all in the same week," he boasted.

With that Eli picked up the other half of his book and peered at the torn page. The first passage he saw was a line the author wrote and, with quivering lips, read it aloud. "If you continue to love Jesus, nothing much can go wrong with you, and I hope you may always do so."

"I know you feel pretty low right now, little man, but his words are true. You are not alone."

With that, Eli began to pick up his other belongings.

"I know a thing or two about Mr. Lewis. I know this book of yours gives excellent advice to novice writers. What a great place for you to start." The old man leaned forward and spoke quietly as if others might hear, "You know he began writing at a young age. He was at least eight when he began to record his thoughts in his journal. How old are you?"

Not interested in carrying on a conversation, Eli answered with brevity, "I'm nine."

"You've got a bit of catching up to do, huh? But I know you can do it. Would you care for ice tea?"

Eli smiled and nodded his head.

"Good, I've grown accustomed to the iced down version... change can be good." The old man directed him to the patio and where a round glass pitcher and several glasses were placed. "I always have my tea this time of day under my willow. Now you go have a seat and I will be with you shortly."

The old man went to the back of the yard, to a tiny stone building covered with ivy and other green vines. The structure would have been completely hidden had the old man not brought attention to it. Eli thought it was a fancy tool shed. He gulped down his drink and massaged his cheek.

Eli sat and looked at the man's yard. It was full of ornaments and statues. In the center of the yard was a tiny pond that bubbled water from a large round sculpture in its center. The yard was thick with vegetation, and a long trellis bore grape vines. A stone wall framed the yard, and butted up to the small stone cottage to which the old man retreated.

The rustic wooden door creaked as the old man emerged with a dusty book. He walked over to where Eli sat. The old man made himself comfortable, poured his glass half full and took the smallest of sips. With deliberation, he thumbed through the brittle pages of the old book.

"Eureka. Here it is."

Startled, Eli furrowed his brow looking at the man. The old man began to read. 'Whenever you are fed up with life, start writing: ink is the great cure for all human ills, as I have found out long ago.' That was written for this very day. The title of this book is *The Letters of C.S. Lewis to Arthur Greeves*, and the passage I read to you, Mr. Lewis wrote in May 30, 1916—ninety years ago to the day. This is my gift to you."

"Wow!" I don't even know you—my mom probably won't let me have it."

"Don't you worry about your mum; it's yours."

"Thank you."

As Eli placed the book on the table he saw on the title page an inscription. "Who is Richard Stanford?"

"You're looking at him."

"You met C.S. Lewis?

"In the flesh. I happened to have heard him lecture at Oxford. I knew he met other writers at the Eastgate Hotel, on occasion. With book in hand,

I approached him at the entrance when he left the building."

"Wow. You met an author—YOU MET C.S. LEWIS!"

"I was happy to make his acquaintance. Since that time I have been fortunate to meet other authors. I have been equally fortunate to meet you, Mr. Eli."

The boy smiled and asked, "Are you a writer?"

Holding back a smile, the old man acknowledged the boy. "I spent many hours writing in that cottage behind us. I taught literature for years at a university nearby. However I am sad to say that I have not written in many years." The old man looked down to the grass.

Dr. Stanford chose the vocation of teaching. Although he was at ease teaching college students, he valued the perspective of the innocence of his new friend, and knew his fragile spirit was formed like that of a hatchling's feather. As a teacher, he knew how delicate his job could be. Not rocket science—just more important, he would muse. At one time, he taught with a spirit that was uniquely his own. He was true to himself, giving his students a glimpse of something real, and he awoke inspiration in his students. A simple assignment, as he told his colleagues, could give life to a seed, make it grow with vigor and blossom in its own incarnation.

Dr. Stanford gave Eli an assignment. He told him to begin writing a journal.

"Begin tonight, Eli. Write from your heart, one moment at a time. Never back away from what you find there."

"I will, but will you?

"Will I what?"

"Write a journal."

Pleasantly tipped off balance, the old man responded with little thought, "Yes, I too shall write a journal."

That night Eli began his journal:

May 30, 2006

Letters to Dr. Stanford
I met a writer today. I had tea with a writer today. I became a
writer today. These moments will sit in my heart as long as I live.

In his cottage, Dr. Stanford wrote:
May 30, 2006
Letters to Eli
"It would be wonderful if moments could be stretched over a life-
time.
"He declared to me, with bold style, his intention to become a
writer, pen the great American novel and within a week of complet-
ing his work, he would have it published. Seldom does one hear
these words uttered by a nine-year-old boy. But actions born
through innocence of the heart are by far the essence of sincerity.

"Children are boundless and limitless with thought, though always
brimming with questions. They write with the eyes of their souls
and the ears of their hearts. They take chances. Not just in their
writing, but in all things they do, their imagination moves them,
not knowing where the road will take them, and they care not.
Unadulterated and uninhibited, they act without worry, and use
their imagination for guidance along the way.

You must not veer off this road, and this moment. Refuse to allow
this to be to be the last time you will take this path of bold declara-
tion and unswerving vision. Of course, most of us do jump off this
course for something else that is safe and makes a tad more money.
My dream, this time, matters not. But I clutch to a hope. That
dear hope is that you, Eli, always remember that, if those on the
side of the road hurl obstacles, which, at some time in your life they
will, you will remember what it was like to be nine again, and want
to be published by week's end."

The great man is one who never loses his child's heart.
— Mencius

It had long since come to my attention that people of
accomplishment rarely sat back and let things happen to
them. They went out and happened to things.

– Leonardo da Vinci

———⊗⊗⊗———

Change is growth. Sameness is death. But without one, we cannot have the other. Always grow, hope and aspire.

———⊗⊗⊗———

KIN

With all things and in all things, we are relatives.

-- Sioux

They wanted a family that was curious, questioning and imaginative. Willie's mom and dad grew up in a black and white world. They, however, cherished their own families, as they recognized they gained much from their upbringing. But starting their own family, they consciously pulled the best pieces from their past to meld with inventions for their new family.

Everything about Willie was green and crisp. He was the kind of kid who made a room glow by his mere presence. He was seven, and the world was his street block and his school sitting on the edge of his neighborhood. Children are vessels to be filled. The thoughts that swirled under his brown mop kept him thinking of questions, just as most children his age. But Willie chased a question with an investigation. His plain thinking led to a mix of ideas, moving him to simple resolve questions. His lily-white face with faint freckles was a beacon, as others gravitated to him. He couldn't help but stick his tongue through the small space between his teeth when he had a mind to. All fifty-one inches and fifty-nine pounds stayed in motion, keeping pace with his curiosity.

It was a rare Saturday evening. It was quiet. Willie's dad took care of kitchen clean-up duties after a meat loaf dinner. Getting comfortable in the family room, his dad sat back, put his feet up and grabbed a novel he had been reading off and on for several weeks. Willie's mom popped in a CD she bought earlier in the day and joined him on the sofa, and she too picked up a book. Willie sat squarely in the middle of floor, in front of the couple play-ing with two sets of Tinker Toys, one new, and one bought two decades earlier for his dad. All the pieces, new and old, were interchangeable. The old, colorless wooden parts connected with the new colorful plastic ones. The pieces from two worlds joined as if they were one, and the hybrid windmill that Willie constructed twirled the same way, as he blew into it much as the one he built completely with new pieces next to it. He busily tested different parts, and slowly constructed with his hands what was going on in his head.

Quietly, Willie's mom said, "Honey, I'm so glad he isn't into all those video games yet. Just look at him. He's having a good time with sticks and wheels."

"You're right. I'm sure he'll be into that other stuff soon enough... I wonder what the next one will be like?" He grinned and gently patted his wife's enlarged tummy.

A few moments passed and Willie's mom, mindful of the time said, "Willie it's time for a bath. We've got church tomorrow."

"Do I have ta?"

"You heard your mother," his dad said sternly.

Keeping his eyes fixed on his craft, and repositioning so he was lying on his stomach, with his knees bent and his bare feet swayed back and forth, he asked, "can I take a shower—I'm getting too old for baths?"

Willie's parents looked at each other and chuckled.

Willie flipped over onto his back with his arms stretched to the ceiling, still fitting pieces of his toy together. Out of the blue Willie interjected, "If Adam and Eve were the first people on earth, then we are related to my best friend, Tommy. Right, Dad?"

Scratching the back of his neck and looking to Willie's mom for telepathic help he answered, "well, that's a good point, young man. I believe you are right."

"That means we're related to everyone, and not just Uncle George and Aunt Karla and gramps and grandpa." He paused and his parents could see the cogs reeling in his head.

In a flash, Willie sat up with his legs folded under him and pensively added, "Gosh we're related to a lot of people who I don't even know... does that mean we're related to Mr. Wong next door?"

"Well, I guess it means just that," said his dad.

Beginning to pick up the Tinker Toys and, at first dropping them one by one into the cardboard cylinder to hear the ping as they struck the metal bottom, he asked more questions. *PING!*

"How about my bus driver, Mr. Louis?" *PING!* Without waiting for an answer from his father or mother, he rattled off a number of people, including Mrs. Weinstein, his teacher. "So let me get this straight. We are all in the same family." *PING!*

They leaned forward, watching their son, and nodded with affirmation.

Willie gained energy with each new thought fueled by his parents support. "This is really cool," said Willie. The Tinker Toy cans were fairly full as he sped up his efforts.

Willie's parents knew he was on to something and that this was a conversation they knew they would continue in the days ahead, as Willie was one to explore. Brought on by his own reasoning, his mom and dad liked what they saw in their young son, and hoped his curiosity and questions would continue his entire life.

"I'm going upstairs to lay out your pj's, and you can take a shower instead of a bath," Willie's mom proclaimed.

But at that moment, his transition from bath to shower was suddenly less important, and Willie spoke up with concern and some doubt.

"Dad?"

"Yes Willie."

"Mr. Wong's eyes slant and Mr. Louis has dark skin... Mrs. Weinstein goes to a different church than we do."

"Yes son, you're right on all three accounts."

Stuffing the last of the Tinker Toys in the canister, he sat in deep thought. Preoccupied and sullen, Willie asked, "then, Dad, how can we be related after all? I mean if we all came from the same place why do we look different or believe in different things from each other?"

Cutting to the chase, his very real question seemed to throw a roadblock in front of his own thinking. His dad's reassuring manner was not enough for Willie, as he wanted answers.

Willie's dad saw displeasure on his son's face and felt his confusion. Like a roller coaster, Willie was up one minute and down the next. So, knowing his son, he came up with a plan. With enthusiasm, he sat down on the floor with Willie and reached out for his hand, "Hey, buddy boy, what you need to do is a little investigative work. This way you can make the decision yourself."

Looking up to his dad, he tilted his head and asked, "what do you mean, Dad? Like 'Mission Impossible?'"

"Well, sort of. Let me explain. Why don't you ask Mr. Wong, Mr. Louis and Mrs. Weinstein the same questions and, depending on what you learn, you will have the evidence to make up your own mind."

The little boy thought of the big idea with trepidation. Willie's dad knew he'd be okay asking honest questions of these three people, as Willie often talked about them with great admiration. But with another nudge from his dad, he reluctantly said he'd give it a shot.

The following day, the sun was bright, and the day was warm. Willie's dad saw Mr. Wong pulling weeds in his yard that afternoon, and urged Willie to go talk with him. Willie, having second thoughts, paused, looked up at his dad and said nothing.

"Willie, you don't have to, but I bet once you start talking, your nervousness will go away—just like last year's spring performance at your school."

Thinking about how he memorized his lines, stood up on stage, looked at all those people and then talked into the microphone, Willie found confidence to talk to Mr. Wong. He walked out the door and meandered over to Mr. Wong's yard.

"Hi Mr. Wong."

"Hello Willie. What do you know?"

"Well, I know I want to ask you a question."

Mr. Wong straightened out from his squatting position. He wiped his face with a towel he pulled from his belt.

"If it's about gardening, I'm the wrong person to ask—too many weeds; just too many weeds. I can't get rid of them."

"No sir it's not about gardening. It's about something else."

"Okay, I'll do my best. What's your question?"

With some vacillation, Willie got up his nerve and asked, "Do you think we're related? I mean, if we all came from the same place, how come we look different?"

Mr. Wong smiled, "Oh I understand. But you asked two questions. Both are very good and I have answers. I say yes, we are related—all of us. We all come from the same place, so we are all connected. That's what related means. You understand?"

Willie nodded politely, needing more.

"Now let me answer your second question. I look different from you, but you look different from your grandma, don't you?

A smile whisked across Willie's face. His chubby cheeks pushed up the outside of his eyes and he said, "yes, you're right about that, Mr. Wong."

"With that big smile you, look a lot like me," laughed Mr. Wong. Mr. Wong then squatted down to Willie's size and said, "Look into my eyes, Willie."

Willie wasn't used to such a request, but did his very best to look at Mr. Wong's eyes.

"No Willie you're looking around my eyes—look directly into my eyes."

Willie focused on Mr. Wong's brown eyes.

"Do you see any difference from your eyes, or your mom's, or anyone else's?"

"Ah... not really," said Willie.

"What's around my eyes doesn't matter, just like your smile a few minutes ago. My eye is round and brown, just like yours. What you see in *my* eyes is what counts. Do you follow me?"

"Yes I do," Willie said with self-assurance.

"Now, young man, would you like to help pull some weeds?"

Like any seven-year-old, for a short time, Willie helped Mr. Wong in his garden.

The next day, Willie stood at his bus stop thinking about his question. Feeling mostly confident, he watched the school bus pull up and stop with a sharp screech. The door slowly opened. He bounded up the steps with enthusiasm, like most days, said hello to Mr. Louis, and sat in his usual seat—the front seat to the right of the driver. After all the children were picked up and brought to school, Willie stayed in his seat on the bus to ask his question. Mr. Louis saw that he didn't budge from his seat, and spoke up.

"What's up, little Willie? Don't want to go to school today?" asked Mr. Louis, in his deep resonant voice.

Instead of answering his question, Willie blurted out, "Mr. Louis, we're related, right? I mean we all come from Adam and Eve…"

Stunned by the questions, Mr. Louis got up from his seat and sat down next to Willie.

Mr. Louis stroked his clean-shaved chin and smiled. "I'm glad you asked that. For a minute I thought you were going to ask me something hard… oh, yes, we are definitely related," Mr. Louis said, and then paused for a few seconds before continuing. In a sure and steady manner, Mr. Louis said, "see, Willie, our souls are all made by God—each and everyone. If God makes all our souls, there's no doubt in my mind that we are all brothers and sisters. It doesn't matter who you are; it matters if you find that soul he gave us. Don't you think?"

"I do Mr. Louis, but why are you black and why am I white?"

"Another good question. Son, It doesn't matter what you look like on the outside," Mr. Louis said. "I bet no one has ever seen the human soul—I suspect it doesn't have a color at all. You're a good boy, and I thank you for calling me kin. Little brother, you best be getting along."

Willie scratched his head and, as he looked into Mr. Louis's brown eyes, they both smiled.

Later that day during recess, and with even greater confidence, he suddenly ran away from his playmates and approached Mrs. Weinstein. Sensing something was different, she reached her hand out and Willie placed his small soft hand into hers.

"Hello Willie. Is everything all right? How come you quit the kickball game? You love kickball."

"Well, I have a question, and thought it would be a good time, with the others out there playing."

They walked over to a wooden bench together and sat down. Willie looked to his favorite teacher and she smiled. Looking at him with her round, blue eyes, he thought of the others he spoke with.

"Are you okay?" Mrs. Weinstein asked.

"Yes, ma'am, but I have an important question to ask you."

"Yes, go ahead. What's your question?"

Are we related?

"How do you mean, Willie?"

"Well if Adam and Eve were the first ones here, we have to be from the same family."

Pleasantly surprised by her young pupil's curiosity, she answered at once, "of course we're all related, Willie. We just don't take time to think about it. That is a very good question and thought. We should always remember that we are all part of the same family."

"But Mrs. Weinstein, you go to a different church than we do. You must believe in something different."

"Ah, yes. I do go to a different place to worship. Let me put it this way. If you believe, and have faith in our Creator, we are all related. Don't you show love and devotion for your mother in different ways than for your father or your grandparents?"

The little boy nodded.

She continued, "celebrations take on many different forms and shapes. I celebrate my love of God in a different way than you, but that doesn't mean we don't all come from one God—from one place."

"Thank you, Mrs. Weinstein. I think you are right. My dad said that I will figure it out by myself with your help. Now I know for sure we're related."

With great satisfaction, Willie ran off and found his friend Tommy. The recess bell blared. As the children lined up to go back in school, Willie said, "Hey Tommy, did you know we're related?"

Turning around and looking at Willie, Tommy said, "Oh brother, does that mean you want to come over for pizza again tonight?"

———— ∞∞∞ ————

Humankind has not woven the web of life. We are but one thread within it. Whatever we do to the web, we do to ourselves. All things are bound together. All things connect.

– Chief Seattle, Native American

———— ❧ ————

The possibilities are endless. We're connected! We're connected to each other, to the plants to the animals to the universe… to our Creator. Think about it. If this is so, should we be doing something different?

———— ❧ ————

LIFE'S DANCE

It is the sweet, simple things of life which are the real ones after all.

— Laura Ingalls Wilder

Somehow cheated of common sense, Sid and Jacqueline unwittingly lived to the throb of a frenzied pace. A frenzied pace conjures up fluster and anxiety with some. But it really wasn't fluster or anxiety for Sid and Jacqueline; it was their status quo. Because it was so for them, it was so for their children. The reason why was irrelevant, as with every journey there are multiple ways to arrive at any destination. But like robots, Sid and Jacqueline were programmed much like others they knew and admired, who lived parallel lives. They did not question their own way of being, but they acted and reacted, caught in an eddy of lists, events and places to go. They did not see what lay before them; they just did not see.

Over the years, Sid seldom thought of the words his father uttered to Sid the day he and Jacqueline were married. "Take time and think, my boy. Open your eyes to what is of value to you. If you don't, one day you'll open your eyes and poof, like a kick in the rump, you realize that you've missed what's most important."

"Yeah, Dad. Thanks," was all Sid could muster that day. Newly graduated from school, only six months in his first job, and having just moved into a condo, he and Jacqueline were hard-pressed to come up with the monthly mortgage. Sid was sure he was hearing what he thought was his dad's hyperbole once again. But he didn't listen to the message. *That's dad going off again,* he thought.

But that was years ago, two moves since, and three children hence. They lived in a home nestled deep in a cul-de-sac. Shuttling their children back and forth and here to there was a way of life for Sid and Jacqueline. They drove their silver Hummer and slogged ahead in all kinds of weather at all times of the day and well into the night to ensure their children were entertained, amused and, with any luck, spent, by the time they were chauffeured home. Their life was a non-stop flight to an unknown destination. Like a dog that chases its tail, they circled their community, only adding a sheen to the leather seats of their car.

"But what has happened to school buses? I think I remember seeing one somewhere," Sid's dad asked not once, but every time he visited, and asked about the children and school.

"Gramps, everyone knows they still have school buses," little Kyle would say, finishing his point on a high note. Laura completed her little brother's thought saying, "some kids are still forced to ride the bus."

"So no bus rides for you two, huh?"

Sid and Jacqueline were not alone as they joined other parents on the misguided path to becoming the best parents they could be. They thought, by extending numerous opportunities to their children, they were up there with the best. Those opportunities, otherwise keeping them occupied, could be one or a mix of many activities and places to send their children, whether they wanted to go or not. There were soccer practices, swimming meets, T-Ball games, martial arts classes, play dates at friends, birthday parties, Cub Scout and Brownie meetings, service clubs, after-school programs, and other sports. Activities where they worshiped, as well as youth groups, keep them on a desirable and selected path, they thought. Then, there were dance classes, skating and piano lessons, among a whole host of other sports and instruments they could learn. There were drama clubs and chorus, to mention a few more.

"You're never at home. I'm always talking to the both of you when you're driving someplace—are you sure they are your own kids in the car? I'm thinking they just jump on and jump off like a trolley car." Sid's dad teased, with more sarcasm then lightheartedness. He continued coolly, "where else do the little darlings have to go?" Sid's dad would ask every time he called on the phone and asked about the children.

Preoccupied with his work in front of him, Sid replied, "Dad, now hang on, I'm at home. I'm not driving anywhere."

Relentlessly his dad pressed, "Wonders never cease. But I bet Jacqueline is out and about."

Becoming agitated Sid took a deliberate breath, held back his emotion and matter-of-factly answered, "well... yes, she is. Laura was dropped off at the mall with friends to go to the movies, and then they are going to have lunch and a café latte."

"Aha! Children? These are children, and they go out to lunch and get a café whatchamacallit?" Sid's dad exclaimed.

Wearing a phone in his ear while talking with his dad, Sid happened to be busily completing a registration form for summer camp for his middle child, Christina. He answered his father in a somewhat light tone, "I hate to say it, Dad, but they have a demanding social calendar. We like to keep them busy."

Cold silence came from Sid's dad. "Why do they have this, what did you call it? A demanding social calendar?" Sid thought a moment, and realized his dad didn't see the attempt of humor in his word choice, but before he could answer, his dad started again. "I'll tell you why, because Sid and Jacqueline have allowed them to have such privileges... too many opportunities. Too much! ...nothing wrong with the little ones. It's the parents. Sorry, but I can't stand by any longer without voicing my opinion. Good bye for now." Sid heard a click and a dial tone. *The old man can't stand by any longer without voicing his opinion? What's new?*

But Sid's dad seldom showed his anger, and it left a sick feeling in Sid's gut. He stopped what he was doing and flung his pen across the room. His hand on top of all the camp registration papers on the kitchen table, with a swoosh he wiped the table clean, as each sheet of paper fluttered end-to-end off the table and decorated the floor. He sat alone, shoulders slumped forward at the kitchen table, pondering his father's words.

Sid knew he had taken a detour from a way that was subtly handed down from his parents. It was a supple, porous way that allowed life to seep in. It was different from the extreme or super-sized cadence of today. This leaning was a new one as, years ago, when Sid was coming along, his parents did not see 'opportunities' the same way as Sid and Jacqueline. They wanted him to join a Little League team, and they wanted little Sid to be a scout or - a member of the swim team at the community pool in the summer. That was the extent of it. Sometimes Sid's parents even wanted him and his brothers and sisters to find ways to entertain themselves. Novel as it might sound, he and his brother Nathan built forts and constructed dams in creeks. Occasionally, they were found reading detective or sci-fi books; they read comic books. There were even quiet afternoons of nothing. Those days would last longer, but gave opportunities for Sid to pull out a model airplane he had yet to build, or look at rocks and feel the smooth texture in his thin hand. Finding the right stick for a bat, little Sid would toss that rock up and swing. With any luck he sent that rock over the center field fence marked '410'. The fence was a hedge and a vivid imagination. Or, with another rock of choice, he would cock his arm and hurl it as far as he could at a target, such as a tree or a soda can.

Sitting at the table, still musing about his father's meddling, Sid took his attention to a fond time he would recall periodically, of the time his dad spent time with him building a tree house. His father's assertions echoed in his head. After an hour of sulking, his dad's passionate words motivated him to do something. He told himself he would spend more time with his children. He would start with his youngest child, Tyler, and try to repeat the experience that he had with his own dad.

That next weekend Sid headed to the internet and researched tree houses. Once he found the right plans for the tree house that struck a chord with him, he printed it off to examine. Meticulously, he wrote a list of everything he needed to build this miniature castle. He went to Home Depot and *bought wood and supplies. Tyler's going to remember this for the rest of his life,* Sid thought.

Once home, his excitement escalated, as he could dust the spider webs off his never-used circular saw and nail gun. Thinking back, Sid's father's rusty saw and banged-up hammer were no longer an option, although they sat in his garage, as Sid's dad now lived in a small apartment. *It takes too long doing it the old-fashioned way.*

He began building a tree house for his first grader. The little boy sat eating a popsicle, paying more attention to the neighbor's dog behind the picket fence than to his dad, who did little to engage his son in the process. After two full weekends, and the evenings in between, the tree house was completed. Sid's mother's uncanny knack to unearth the right, perhaps aged and dusty curtains found in a dry rotted box in the attic, wasn't even considered. Jacqueline decorated the edifice with colorful furnishings from Target, and declared the residence now ready for occupancy.

"It took longer the old way, and was much more difficult, but one thing was for sure: that old tree house wasn't nearly as pretty as this baby," Sid declared to Jacqueline. That never mattered to Sid before, but for some reason it mattered that day. Sid, with excitement, got down on his knees and wrapped his arm around his son's shoulders. "We did it, Tyler, we did it! How do you like it?" Turning from his gaze at the tree house and looking squarely in his son's eyes, he realized the most important ingredient was missing. It was too late and his sinking feeling was that his son didn't feel a part of the experience. He didn't seem to care it was done. *The tree house isn't the thing. I blew it… it's not the thing that matters*, Sid thought.

Like an arrow, a thought came swiftly back to Sid's consciousness. *Take time and think… one day you'll open your eyes and, poof, you come to realize that you've missed what's most important.* His dad's words came back to him in that instant.

Sid moped for days. He felt scared. He knew what was most important, and thinking that it could go "poof" did not sit well with him. But the family's frenetic pace kept him from thinking about it too long, and life stayed about the same for him and his family.

Many strip malls in America are anchored by Gold's Gym, a Chinese restaurant, a Starbucks and a dance studio. Sid's fourteen-year-old daughter took dance lessons and, by her teacher's account, was very good. Sid knew nothing about dancing, and began an education about dance and more when Jacqueline signed Laura up for the class six months before the tree house fiasco.

By taking Laura to dance practice once a week for several months, Sid learned that dancers don leotards and ballet slippers, file into these nondescript buildings and learn ballet, modern dance, jazz and tap. What Sid didn't realize that, once there, his daughter and others could focus on themselves and, deep within, they knew they were graceful and beautiful. Even for a fleeting moment, all dancers think of what it would be like to one day dance for and in front of others and finish to an ovation and being handed a bouquet of flowers—what a moment. Sid wasn't thinking at this level, and viewed his daughter's time with dance as yet another opportunity for socialization and exercise. He hoped, too, that she would enjoy and appreciate the nuances, but this ephemeral thought never came to be at the forefront of Sid's mind.

The reality of it was that Sid and Jacqueline looked at dance as yet just another activity to keep their daughter busy, and to provide them with some exercise. Many winter days, full of blustery winds and chilling rains, made a difficult setting for Laura to ready herself for dance. Jacqueline would not let this get in their way, and she reluctantly went to dance. The beauty of the activity was seldom a thought, as Jacqueline and Sid pulled their daughter away from the television to transport her to dance.

Sid would pick her up from dance and, as if on autopilot, he asked her how her hour was.

"Fine, Dad! You always ask me that," she said with teenage attitude.

"I know I ask that all the time but 'is fine', is that all you can tell me?"

"Yeah, it was fine. Fine, *fine*, fine."

"Do you like dancing?"

"Yeah, it's fine."

Months passed since the first dance class and all was 'fine' over those months for Laura. The annual recital was the pinnacle of the year, and was that month. The program was held at a local college in their main auditorium. The costume they purchased for their daughter was satin and dotted with sequins. With the immense preparation, Sid began to think about this event and how special it must really be.

The night of the recital, much was the same in the house. Everyone frenetically scurried to get to the auditorium, and Laura to the dressing room. As Sid found his seat, he waited for Jacqueline to join him from the dressing room. He read the program from cover to cover and was amazed.

"How did all these kids fit into that studio each week?" He said to a parent sitting next to him. "This is a huge production."

When the curtain went up, Sid was in awe. As each new dance troupe entered, performed and exited, he was captivated at the beauty and grace of these young people. Their energy, their precision and their smiles told stories. When his daughter's class took the stage, Sid was mesmerized. Their movements blended in such a way that both good and bad were appreciated and Sid would never know the difference.

Laura was good. She was beautiful. She told him the truth. She *was* fine.

Sid saw her with fresh eyes. Many recent events began seeping into his consciousness. *It's not hauling them here and there and dumping them off for opportunities*, he thought. *It's not 'doing' for them or building something for them.*

At intermission, the parent Sid spoke to earlier volunteered, "Wow, which was wonderful. You really need to take time and think about life— most of us don't, ya know? I mean, it is right in front of us. For me, it is good to be reminded that, if you don't keep your eyes wide open, its like, poof, and you've missed what's most important."

Sid was stunned and looked at the man. "You're right. I've heard that from someone before." The stranger nodded with a smile.

In the frenzied pace of his well-intentioned life, Sid rarely took the time to see beauty that his children offered each day. He was caught in a whirlpool, repeating the same motions, looking for new answers.

Jacqueline asked Sid to hand Laura a bouquet of roses she hid in the back of the car. He offered her the flowers with a smile. On the drive home, during a rare quiet moment, Sid thought about the rusty saw, the dusty curtains, and what was important in another lifetime is still important today.

People travel to wonder at the height of mountains, at the huge waves of the sea, at the long course of rivers, at the vast compass of the ocean, at the circular motion of the stars; and they pass by themselves without wondering.
                                                    – St. Augustine

Many eyes go through the meadow, but few see the flowers.

— Ralph Waldo Emerson

———∞———

What's close seem miles away. But we yearn for what we see in the distance. The beauty of our essence, our soul, is boundless but we overlook it. We should attempt to listen without speaking and without clutter in our mind. If we're silent we hear the quiet. We will hear something in the quiet. We will see something if we are open to seeing.

The flowers are pretty, so now we should just take a look. It's rather simple.

———∞———

LISTENING TO OTHERS

Quotations

THE JOURNEY

Mountains should be climbed with as little effort as possible and without desire, the reality of your own nature should determine the speed. If you become restless, speed up. If you become winded, slow down, you climb the mountain in an equilibrium between restlessness and exhaustion. Then, when you're no longer thinking ahead, each footstep isn't just a means to an end but a unique event in itself.
— Robert Pirsig

In rivers, the water that you touch is the last of what has passed and the first of that which comes; so with present time.
— Leonardo da Vinci

It's taken me all my life to learn what not to play.
— Dizzy Gillespie

Our life is a long and arduous quest after the truth and the soul requires inward restfulness to attain its full height.
— Mahatma Gandhi

May your trails be crooked, winding, lonesome, dangerous, leading to the most amazing view. May your mountains rise into and above the clouds.
— Edward Abbey

TODAY

Never let yesterday use up too much of today.
                                                    − Will Rogers

*The past, the present and the future are really one: they
are today.*
                                                    − Harriet Beecher Stowe

The future starts today, not tomorrow.
                                                    − Pope John Paul II

*Learn from yesterday, live for today, hope for tomorrow.
The important thing is not to stop questioning.*
                                                    − Albert Einstein

Carpe diem, quam minimum credula postero.
*Translation: Seize today, and put as little trust as you
can in the morrow.*
                                                    − Horace

KNOWLEDGE AND WISDOM

Seek Wisdom, not knowledge. Knowledge is of the past, wisdom is of the future.

– Lumbee saying

Knowledge comes, but wisdom lingers.

– Alfred Lord Tennyson

As soon as a man does not take his existence for granted, but he holds it as something unfathomably mysterious, thought begins.

– Albert Schweitzer

To know that you know, and to know that you don't know—that is the real wisdom.

– Confucius

DOUBT

Modest doubt is called the beacon of the wise.
                                    – William Shakespeare

Believing hath a core of unbelieving.
                                    – Robert Williams Buchanan

Laugh at yourself, but don't ever aim your doubt at yourself. Be bold. When you embark for strange places, don't leave any of yourself safely on shore. Have the nerve to go into unexplored territory.
                                    – Alan Alda

DETERMINATION

Self help is the best help.   Heaven helps those who help themselves.
> – Aesop - Hercules and the Wagoner

One of the things I learned the hard way was that it does-n't' pay to get discouraged. Keeping busy and making optimism a way of life can restore your faith in yourself.
> – Lucille Ball

What saves a man is to take a step. Then another step.
> – C.S. Lewis

It's all about the attitude, gut, heart and determination to go out and give 120% every time to try and help the team win.
> – Bo Jackson

Yes we can.
> – Barack Obama

FAITH AND HOPE

Hope is the thing with feathers
That perches in the soul.
And sings the tune
Without the words,
And never stops at all.

       – Emily Dickinson

While there's life, there's hope.

       – Cicero

Faith has to do with things that are not seen and hope
with things that are not at hand.

       – Saint Thomas Aquinas

Optimism is the faith that leads to achievement. Nothing
can be done without hope and confidence.

       – Helen Keller

Believe in yourself! Have faith in your abilities! Without a
humble but reasonable confidence in your own powers you
cannot be successful or happy.

       – Norman Vincent Peale

Not truth, but faith, it is that keeps the world alive.

       – Edna St. Vincent Millay

To disbelieve is easy; to scoff is simple; to have faith is
harder.

       – Louis L'Amour

GENTLENESS

The greatest strength is gentleness.

— Iroquois saying

Only the weak are cruel. Gentleness can only be expected from the strong.

— Leo Buscaglia

Nothing is so strong as gentleness, nothing so gentle as real strength.

— Saint Francis de Sales

Gentleness is the antidote for cruelty.

— Pjaedrus

Nothing is so strong as gentleness and nothing is so gentle as real strength.

— Ralph W. Stockman

PEACE

While I thought that I was learning how to live, I have been learning how to die.

— Leonardo da Vinci

Death is more universal than life; everyone dies but not everyone lives.
Do not fear death so much, but rather the inadequate life.

— From "The Mother" by Bertolt Brecht

Peace comes from within. Do not seek it without.

— Buddha

There can never be peace between nations until there is first known that true peace which is within the souls of men.

— Black Elk- Native American

For where your treasure is, there will your heart be also.

— The Bible, Matthew 6:21

SELF

Those who would mend other, should first mend themselves.
— Aesop — "The Quack Toad

Seek not good from without; seek it within yourself or you will never find it.
— Epictetus

Ye shall know the truth, and the truth shall make you free.
— The Bible, John 8:32

You only grow when you are alone.
— Paul Newman

If we lose love and self respect for each other, this is how we finally die.
— Maya Angelou

There are three things extremely hard: steel, a diamond, and to know one's self.
— Benjamin Franklin

When wealth is lost, nothing is lost; when health is lost, something is lost; when character is lost, all is lost.
— Billy Graham

Friendship with ones self is all important, because without it one cannot be friends with anyone else in the world.
— Eleanor Roosevelt

INTROSPECTION

The night wind with the big dark curves of the night sky in it, the night wind gets inside of me and understands all of my secrets.

– Carl Sandburg

Who looks outside, dreams; who looks inside, awakes.

– Carl Jung

I was always looking outside myself for strength and confidence, but it comes from within. It is there all the time.

– Anna Freud

We forge gradually our greatest instrument for understanding the world - introspection. We discover that humanity may resemble us very considerably - that the best way of knowing the inwardness of our neighbors is to know ourselves.

– Walter Lippmann

The philosophy of the wisest man that ever existed, is mainly derived from the act of introspection.

– William Godwin

Introspection and preserved writings give us far more insight into the ways of past humans than we have into the ways of past dinosaurs. For that reason, I'm optimistic that we can eventually arrive at convincing explanations for these broadest patterns of human history.

– Jared Diamond

ON BEING HUMAN

We are what we believe we are.
> – C.S. Lewis

We can live without religion and meditation, but we cannot survive without human affection.
> – Dalai Lama

All I can say about life is, Oh God, enjoy it!
> – Bob Newhart

The essence of being human is that one does not seek perfection.
> – George Orwell

A human being is a deciding being.
> – Viktor E. Frankl

The ideas that have lighted my way have been kindness, beauty and truth.
> – Albert Einstein

You don't have a soul. You are a Soul. You have a body.
> – C.S. Lewis

The mind is never satisfied with the objects immediately before it, but is always breaking away from the present moment, and losing itself in schemes of future felicity... The natural flights of the human mind are not from pleasure to pleasure, but from hope to hope.
> – Samuel Johnson

GIVING

God gave us each a song.

— Ute saying

Nothing that you have not given away will ever be really yours.

— C.S. Lewis

For it is in giving that we receive.

— St. Francis of Assisi

Time and money spent in helping men to do more for themselves is far better than mere giving.

— Henry Ford

Pity may represent little more than the impersonal concern which prompts the mailing of a check, but true sympathy is the personal concern which demands the giving of one's soul.

— Martin Luther King Jr.

I had found a kind of serenity, a new maturity... I didn't feel better or stronger than anyone else but it seemed no longer important whether everyone loved me or not - more important now was for me to love them. Feeling that way turns your whole life around; living becomes the act of giving.

— Beverly Sills

Let us not be satisfied with just giving money. Money is not enough, money can be got, but they need your hearts to love them. So, spread your love everywhere you go.

— Mother Teresa

SIMPLICITY AND LIVING ORDINARILY

Mental toughness is many things. It is humility because it behooves all of us to remember that simplicity is the sign of greatness and meekness is the sign of true strength. Mental toughness is spartanism with qualities of sacrifice, self-denial, dedication. It is fearlessness, and it is love.
— Vince Lombardi

Human subtlety will never devise an invention more beautiful, more simple or more direct than does Nature, because in her inventions, nothing is lacking and nothing is superfluous. Simplicity is the ultimate sophistication.
— Leonardo da Vinci

Simplicity in character, in manners, in style; in all things the supreme excellence is simplicity.
— Henry Wadsworth Longfellow

There is no greatness where there is no simplicity, goodness and truth.
— Leo Tolstoy

All great change in America begins at the dinner table.
— Ronald Reagan

Simplicity is the final achievement. After one has played a vast quantity of notes and more notes, it is simplicity that emerges as the crowning reward of art.
— Frederic Chopin

It's true. I'm a simple person. Some people tend to live from trauma to trauma, and that energizes them. I have a hectic schedule, but my mind seeks simplicity - like being in nature, a long bike ride, or sitting on the back porch.

— Amy Grant

Take care of the little things and the big things will take care of themselves.

— Aesop -The Astrologer

What we have to learn to do, we learn doing.

— Aristotle

HAPPINESS

Be content with your lot.
    – Aesop - "The Fox and the Crab"

Happiness is when what you think, what you say, and what you do are in harmony.
    – Mahatma Gandhi

There is no value in life except what you choose to place upon it and no happiness in any place except what you bring to it yourself.
    – Henry David Thoreau

Happiness can exist only in acceptance.
    – George Orwell

To enjoy good health, to bring true happiness to one's family, to bring peace to all, one must first discipline and control one's own mind. If a man can control his mind he can find the way to Enlightenment, and all wisdom and virtue will naturally come to him.
    – Buddha

Many persons have a wrong idea of what constitutes true happiness. It is not attained through self-gratification but through fidelity to a worthy purpose.
    – Helen Keller

Happiness is not a goal; it is a by-product.
    – Eleanor Roosevelt

IMAGINATION

Everything you can imagine is real.
— Pablo Picasso

Imagination is more important than knowledge.
— Albert Einstein

Reason is the natural order of truth; but imagination is the organ of meaning.
— C.S. Lewis

COMPASSION

Our own brain, our own heart is our temple; the philosophy is kindness.

— Dalai Lama

Forget injuries, never forget kindnesses.

— Confucius

The individual is capable of both great compassion and great indifference. He has it within his means to nourish the former and outgrow the latter.

— Norman Cousins

I believe that man will not merely endure. He will prevail. He is immortal, not because he alone among creatures has an inexhaustible voice, but because he has a soul, a spirit capable of compassion and sacrifice and endurance.

— William Faulkner

The whole idea of compassion is based on a keen awareness of the interdependence of all these living beings, which are all part of one another, and all involved in one another.

— Thomas Merton

TRUTH

Whatever is, is right.

– Alexander Pope

We can easily forgive a child who is afraid of the dark; the real tragedy of life is when men are afraid of the light.

– Plato

From the evening breeze to this hand on my shoulder, everything has its truth.

– Albert Camus

Let anyone among you who is without sin be the first to throw a stone.

– Jesus

HUMILITY

We often make much of the ornamental and despise the useful.
— Aesop, "The Stag and His Reflection"

Humility must always be the portion of any man who receives acclaim earned in the blood of his followers and the sacrifices of his friends.
— Dwight D. Eisenhower

Humility is the foundation of all the other virtues hence, in the soul in which this virtue does not exist there cannot be any other virtue except in mere appearance.
— Saint Augustine

Power is dangerous unless you have humility.
— Richard J. Daley

There is no gardening without humility. Nature is constantly sending even its oldest scholars to the bottom of the class for some egregious blunder.
— Alfred Clayton

FRIENDSHIP

*Don't walk behind me; I may not lead. Don't walk in
front of me; I may not follow. Walk beside me that we
may be as one.*

– Ute saying

Friendship is a single soul dwelling in two bodies.

– Aristotle

The only way to have a friend is to be one.

– Ralph Waldo Emerson

*I have friends in overalls whose friendship I would not
swap for the favor of the kings of the world.*

– Thomas A. Edison

*But friendship is precious, not only in the shade, but in the
sunshine of life, and thanks to a benevolent arrangement
the greater part of life is sunshine.*

– Thomas Jefferson

KINDNESS

No act of kindness, no matter how small, is ever wasted.
                    — Aesop, "The Lion and the Mouse"

Human kindness has never weakened the stamina or soft-ened the fiber of a free people. A nation does not have to be cruel to be tough.
                    — Franklin D. Roosevelt

Kindness is more important than wisdom, and the recogni-tion of this is the beginning of wisdom.
                    — Theodore Isaac Rubin

Kindness and faithfulness keep a king safe, through kind-ness his throne is made secure.
                    — King Solomon

Kindness is the language which the deaf can hear and the blind can see.
                    — Mark Twain

That best portion of a man's life, his little, nameless, unre-membered acts of kindness and love.
                    — William Wordsworth

FORGIVENESS

Forgiveness is the key to action and freedom.
— Hannah Arendt

Life is an adventure in forgiveness.
— Norman Cousins

Forgiveness is the answer to the child's dream of a miracle by which what is broken is made whole again, what is soiled is made clean again.
— Dag Hammarskjold

To err is human; to forgive, divine.
— Alexander Pope

He that cannot forgive others breaks the bridge over which he must pass himself; for every man has need to be forgiven.
— Thomas Fuller

LOVE

There is no remedy for love but to love more.
— Henry David Thoreau

Love takes up where knowledge leaves off.
— Saint Thomas Aquinas

To love another person is to see the face of God.
— Victor Hugo

Love sought is good, but given unsought, is better.
— William Shakespeare

The greatest pleasure of life is love.
— Euripides

Love has features which pierce all hearts, he wears a bandage which conceals the faults of those beloved. He has wings, he comes quickly and flies away the same.
— Voltaire

Love is a chain of love as nature is a chain of life.
— Truman Capote

Where there is love there is life.
— Mohandas Gandhi

Without love in you life, you have nothing.
— Wynonna Judd

Love is life. And if you miss love, you miss life.
— Leo Buscaglia

MEDITATION AND PRAYER

You become what you think about all day long.
— Ralph Waldo Emerson

*If you begin to live life looking for the God that is all
around you, every moment becomes a prayer.*
— Frank Bianco

*Prayer for many is like a foreign land. When we go there,
we go as tourists. Like most tourists, we feel uncomfortable
and out of place. Like most tourists, we therefore move on
before too long and go somewhere else.*
— Robert McAfee Brown

*It is the prayer of my innermost being to realize my
supreme identity in the liberated play of consciousness, the
Vast Expanse. Now is the moment, Here is the place of
Liberation.*
— Alex Grey

*Prayer indeed is good, but while calling on the gods a man
should himself lend a hand.*
— Hippocrates

*I like the silent church before the service begins better than
any preaching.*
— Ralph Waldo Emerson

*Prayer is a thought, a belief, a feeling, arising within the
mind of the one praying.*
— Ernest

EXPERIENCES

Human beings, who are almost unique in having the ability to learn from the experience of others, are also remarkable for their apparent disinclination to do so.
— Douglas Adams

If we could sell our experiences for what they cost us, we'd all be millionaires.
— Abigail Van Buren

Life is the art of drawing without an eraser.
— John W. Gardner

Nothing is a waste of time if you use the experience wisely.
— Auguste Rodin

All quotes within this manuscript have been found in publications and the internet and remain the intellectual property of those to whom they have been attributed. Usage of all quotations adheres to the fair use copyright principal.

Share your stories with the author by connecting with him on his web site at www.edwardgkardos.com

About the Author

Ed Kardos and his wife, Kristin, have four children and live in Richmond, Virginia. *Zen Master Next Door* is his latest work. Inspiration for his work comes from his view of spirituality, friendship and our connection to one another and our world. His life's focus, his relationships and desire to listen to his surroundings gave him a unique ability to write these stories. He refers to them as Zen parables because their very nature is to remind us of the values we hold dear and to encourage our own introspection.

Yours, Aiden was his first novel and was published in 2002. His view of spirituality, friendships and connection to the world inspires his writing.

Printed in the United States
140929LV00003B/7/P